Endorsem

Tracy shows determination and perseverance. She gives hope to the hopeless
and those feeling defeated and victimized. I have known Tracy for years
and with everything she has experienced, she has a smile on her face, joy in
her heart, and exudes grace. I believe as people look at Tracy's life and what
she has endured, how God delivered her and the victory she has now, they,
too, will know they can make it through anything and everything. This is
an intriguing book that will capture your attention and draw you into how
you, too, can turn a mess into a message.

—Kathy DeGraw, president and founder of Kathy DeGraw
Ministries, author of *Unshackled*, *Prophetic Spiritual Warfare*,
and *Discerning and Destroying the Works of Satan*

Broken and Blessed is a brave confrontation of sexual abuse, generational
strongholds, and the danger of accepting brokenness as an identity. Tracy's
reconning with her own story is a challenge to each of us to accept where
we've been, reject the lies that threaten to define us, and accept God's power
and presence as our true victory.

—Pastor Aaron Brown, Third Coast Community Church

Broken and Blessed is the epic journey to find and trust God in the midst
of trials and betrayals. Honest and inspiring, the twists and turns in Tracy
Michaud's memoir will have you reading late into the night. This book leads
you to find the joy, faith, and courage to transform the broken pieces of your
life into places of blessing.

—Robyn Dykstra, national Christian women's
speaker and author of *The Widow Wore Pink*

Here is the transparent and moving story about a woman who, facing extraordinary personal tragedy and challenge, never gives up hope and learns to
trust in the God who rescues and empowers. While Tracy's circumstances
may be different, this is the book to read if you are looking for inspiration
and guidance to make it through the hard stuff of life.

—Kevin Pike, senior pastor of the Fearless Family of Churches

Broken and Blessed is an incredible story of redemption and restoration. Author Tracy Michaud took many courageous steps to stop the generational sin that plagued her family. Great faith and grit empowered this sister in Christ to turn a new page and allow the pain of her past to provide purpose in her life. This is one of those stories where the trajectory of Tracy's life illustrates from Romans 8:28 how God worked all things, even the hard things, together for good. He is ALWAYS FAITHFUL!

—Athena Dean Holtz, founder and publisher at
Redemption Press and She Writes for Him

Broken and
BLESSED

Lynn,

LIVE courageously!

Walk by Faith!

♡Tracy

Broken and
BLESSED

How God Set Me Free from
Abuse, Dysfunctional Relationships,
and Generational Sin

TRACY
MICHAUD

REDEMPTION
PRESS

Published by Redemption Press, PO Box 427, Enumclaw, WA 98022.
Toll-Free (844) 2REDEEM (273-3336)

All websites and phone numbers listed herein are accurate at the time of publication but may change in the future or cease to exist. Groups, organizations, websites, and resources are mentioned for informational purposes.

Content warning: This story contains emotional and physical trauma, childhood sexual abuse, and many difficult life situations on the road to inner healing, deliverance, and redemption.

The names of certain persons mentioned in this book have been changed in order to protect the privacy of the individuals involved.

Redemption Press is honored to present this title in partnership with the author. The views expressed or implied in this work are those of the author. Redemption Press provides our imprint seal representing design excellence, creative content, and high-quality production.

Author cover photographs by Cara Williams

Unless otherwise indicated, all Scripture quotations are from the Holy Bible, New International Version®. NIV®. Copyright © 1973, 1978, 1984, 2011 by Biblica, Inc.™ Used by permission. All rights reserved worldwide.

Scripture quotations marked (AMP) are taken from the Amplified Bible, Copyright © 1954, 1958, 1962, 1964, 1965, 1987 by The Lockman Foundation. Used by permission. www.lockman.org.

Scripture quotations marked (AMPC) are taken from the Amplified® Bible (AMPC), Copyright © 1954, 1958, 1962, 1964, 1965, 1987 by The Lockman Foundation. Used by permission. www.lockman.org.

Scripture quotations marked (KJV) are taken from the King James Version of the Bible.

Scripture quotations marked (MSG) are taken from THE MESSAGE, copyright © 1993, 2002, 2018 by Eugene H. Peterson. Used by permission of NavPress. All rights reserved. Represented by Tyndale House Publishers, Inc.

Scripture quotations marked (NKJV) are taken from the New King James Version®. Copyright © 1982 by Thomas Nelson. Used by permission. All rights reserved.

ISBN 13: 978-1-64645-325-2 (Paperback)
978-1-64645-323-8 (ePub)
978-1-64645-324-5 (Mobi)

Library of Congress Catalog Card Number: 2021923969

Dedication

This book is dedicated to my Lord and Savior, Jesus Christ. It is in *you* I place my *hope*. My *joy* comes from recognizing that *you knew everything about me*, Tracy Jane, before I was ever formed. I have great comfort knowing I wasn't a surprise to you. Thank you, Father, for watching over me from birth, saving me, forgiving me, and transforming my life . . . it *has not* been an easy journey.

To my one and only son, Rob, who inspired me to persevere and to be *all* who God created me to be. *You* are the only person in the world I would have rolled into church for. I am forever grateful for your obedience. It saved my life. I love you.

To my husband, Albert, best friend and lover, our life together has been challenging and fulfilling. I am so blessed to be your wife. I love you. You are my rock! God's Word alone has transformed us and has taught us how to be excellent in His eyes, as individuals and together united as *one*. God has been faithful to us as we live for Him and place Him above all. I am forever grateful to Him in restoring and redeeming our lives. He alone gets *all* the glory.

To my sister, Amy Jo, my in-laws, my forever friend and brother-in-law, and my stepdaughters, you have been significant in my life. I would not be the woman I am today without each of you. I love you all.

Contents

Foreword

I am so blessed to write the foreword for this very special book about the life of my precious, godly friend. God brought Tracy into my life when things weren't going so well for her in her personal and spiritual life. Over the years, I have been privileged to see this woman of God blossom, to go from the caterpillar to the butterfly right before my eyes.

The amount of trauma, discouragement, disappointment, chronic pain—emotionally and physically—she has endured in her lifetime is beyond what I could have imagined anyone surviving physically, let alone emotionally and spiritually. God continues to turn things around, and Tracy is a perfect miracle of transformation.

God has a very special anointing and blessing on Tracy. Only God knows the far-reaching effects on those she has met and those she has yet to meet. I know she has blessed my life beyond measure these last twenty years, by her open, loving heart and hunger for God and His Word.

As you read the pages of this book, many times you will gasp. Many times you will cry. Many times you will rejoice. In the end, you will give glory to God for His faithfulness. And, hopefully, have more faith to believe God for the "impossible" in your own life.

With greatest respect for my friend and honor to our Lord,
Rev. Dr. Renee Hibma

Acknowledgments

I am so blessed by the friends God strategically placed in my life to walk alongside me in different seasons.

First, I want to thank Tom Dykstra. You were the first individual to witness the scene of my traumatic car accident. Your assistance saved my life. I am thankful we were able to meet over twenty years later and share a meal. I am forever grateful.

I want to thank Allegan County Sheriff's Office and the police officers who assisted in rescuing me, especially Officer Haverdink. Words cannot express my gratitude to you for restoring my ability to breathe freely on scene as I gasped for air; you literally saved my life. I am forever grateful.

I want to thank Hamilton Fire Department, Mercy Ambulance, Aero Med, John's Auto Service, and all medical personnel involved in my care. I have deep gratitude to you all who give selflessly to assist others; your hearts are appreciated. I am forever grateful.

I want to thank Anita Grant, my favorite nurse. You blessed my life by caring so deeply for me, and you made life fun during the darkest times of being a hospitalized teenage girl.

I want to thank Adina, the hospital chaplain who visited me often, praying with me and contacting Joni. I can still hear your joyful accent.

I want to thank Joni Eareckson Tada. You greatly encouraged me by calling me while I was hospitalized. Your ability to fully understand my situation filled my heart with hope. After our conversation, I knew that God had a plan for my life, and I was to write my story. You have abundantly blessed my life.

I want to thank Rick Allen, my favorite drummer in the whole world. Your kindness and compassion toward me after my amputation truly changed my life. I know you've heard it before but I want to thank you once again for the inspiration you placed deep within me to endure this life as an amputee. Thank you for taking the time to encourage me and for your generosity to my family through the decades. I am forever grateful.

I want to thank my precious friend, Renee. You have always been a godly influence in my life. During our decades of friendship, you have worn many hats. You are gifted beyond measure. I am continually blessed by your wisdom.

My anointed friend and mentor, Kathy. You taught me about true worship and intimacy with our heavenly Father, inner healing, deliverance, and so much more. I am a free woman because of your obedience. I am forever grateful.

My best friend, Katie. You have loved me unconditionally, no matter what. Thank you for believing in me when I struggled through the tears in writing this book. You are always there for me. I love you.

My dear friends Mandi, Sheryl, Jim, and Tammy. You each hold a special place in my heart where words just cannot express my gratitude. I am forever grateful to all of you.

My childhood girlfriends, near and far. I treasure our friendships. Thank you for loving me unconditionally.

Special thanks to Dr. Frank Alfieri, for your compassion and encouragement during the most difficult days I endured with pain. Our family is grateful for yours. I appreciate you.

My beloved prayer warriors, Renee, Gwyn, Dawn, Sheryl, Lisa, Debi, Amanda, and Sue. Thank you for lifting me up to our Father and warring in the Spirit on my behalf. I thank each of you from the bottom of my heart for your prayer covering.

Special thanks to my editor, Jennifer Edwards. I appreciate you for deeply immersing yourself into my life and story, for believing in me when it was difficult, and for pulling me out of my comfort zone in crafting this book for future generations. I am forever grateful.

Special thanks to my Speak Up leader and coach, Robyn Dykstra. I appreciate your guidance and knowledge in all things writing and speaking, and for stretching me beyond comfort. Your smile brings me joy. I am forever grateful for our divine connection.

Special thanks to Athena and the team at Redemption Press. Thank you for assisting me and guiding me through the publishing process to give birth to the book God placed on my heart as a teenage girl. A dream fulfilled. I am forever grateful.

Special thanks to my husband, my son, and my family who encouraged me to move forward with this book no matter what. I love you all.

And finally, to my parents. I would not be here without you. I love you both.

Broken and Blessed

Before I formed you in the womb I knew you
[and approved of you as My chosen instrument],
And before you were born I consecrated you [to Myself as My own];
I have appointed you as a prophet to the nations.

Jeremiah 1:5 (AMP)

BROKEN AND *BLESSED*. THESE TWO WORDS SUM UP MY LIFE. WRITING
this book has not been an easy task, but neither was the darkness I
lived under ever since I was a little girl.

Have you ever felt so defeated in life that your situation seemed
hopeless? Do you find yourself repeating the same vicious cycle of
trying to get unstuck from a bad habit? Do you have traits that resem-
ble your father or mother? Maybe ones you don't like—the dark ones?
We all do. It's likely you can identify some similar behavior in yourself
that was present in your family members long before you came along.
Perhaps you have identical patterns in relational issues, addictions, or
medical diagnoses. Or maybe the same tendencies of betrayal, reacting
out of anger, or abuse. You're not alone. All of us have sin patterns
passed down to us from previous generations.

Generational sin is real. Curses are real. But so are blessings. Most
people, including those in the church, never dig into the root of the
sin problem. We attribute our difficulties to poor choices or fate or the
devil himself. More often than not, you will hear that God is a good
and loving Father, and I wholeheartedly agree that He is. But also, He
is a holy God who disciplines and judges fairly, promising blessings for
those who obey Him, and curses for those who don't (Deuteronomy

17

5:9–10). Those blessings and curses extend down through the generations. Our lives are in His hands, whether we love Him or hate Him.

Looking back over my life, I was destined for defeat. From birth I was unwanted, neglected, and rejected. My mother, in her teens, dabbled in playing with the Ouija board. She became a lover of money and relied on her daily horoscope to guide her life. The Bible is clear in saying, "You shall not bow down to them nor serve them. For I, the LORD your God, am a jealous God, visiting the iniquity of the fathers upon the children to the third and fourth generations of those who hate Me" (Deuteronomy 5:9 NKJV). Our family was godless: full of jealousy, anger, neglect, and deceit. Yet even in the darkness, there were flickers of hope, thanks to the light of some God-believers who were placed in my life.

My story is one of a strong, stubborn, and determined little girl who, despite all earthly odds against her, would not give up or allow life-altering tragedies to change her smile.

For as long as I can remember, I knew Jesus loved me and God was with me. As a toddler, I was often singing "Jesus Loves Me" and saying bedtime prayers as taught by my stepfather, one of my perpetrators. Nighttime often turned to fear for me as bedtime prayers led to inappropriate touching and molestation.

I was emotionally and sexually abused for years and full of shame, anger, and bitterness because my mother knew and did not protect me. I trusted no one, *especially men*. I was full of fear.

Disabled as a teenager due to serious, life-threatening injuries sustained in a car accident, I vowed to take care of myself, at least as well as any teenage girl could be expected to without the guidance of good and godly parents. I led a rebellious and immoral life, feeling unworthy, ashamed, and lacking any sense of joy and peace. The amputation of my leg, which saved my life, left me more insecure and lacking self-acceptance. My entire body was wracked with constant pain. I was deceived, broken, and completely lost. Due to the daily misery I experienced, I finally sought professional help. I was diagnosed with post-traumatic stress disorder (PTSD) and depression-related bipolar

II, and thus was placed on mood-stabilizing medications. I ingested the prescriptions for several years without feeling any different. I was unwilling to reveal my internal struggle with my doctor; it was too awful to talk about.

The truth was grievous. I was living in oppression, under a generational curse that spiraled me down a path to devastation. My life was marked by fear, chaos, hopelessness, infirmity, grief, secrecy, and depression.

I knew that God saw everything. I repeatedly told myself to "never give up" because one day it would all be okay. Although I didn't understand, I truly believed that everything happens for a reason.

Are *you* lost? Are *you* confused? Do *you* long for peace, joy, or contentment in your life? If you have ever felt unworthy, insecure, rejected, or hopeless, *you are not alone*. I want you to know God loves you unconditionally, and He alone can grant you the desires of your heart. He healed me, and He desires to heal you too. God is bigger than any circumstance. Defeat is not an option!

When my second husband and I genuinely repented and surrendered our lives to the Lord, our lives drastically changed. Honestly, it was not easy or fun at times because truth revealed many hard issues that needed to be faced *and* changed. Albert and I were released from the bondage that held us down. However, we were not free of the consequences of our sin. But God, in all His mercy and goodness, bestowed one blessing after another upon us.

Once I discovered who I was in Christ, the shackles and chains that kept me immovable, were unlocked. I was no longer stuck, attached to the burdens that weighed so heavily on me. I was free like the day the traction pins were removed from my physical body. Although I was no longer held in place, the wounds were deep, and many layers of healing had to transpire. My eyes were wide open to the truth about what was really occurring.

Against medical advice, I tossed out the mood-stabilizing medications and trusted God to fully take care of me. While I am not suggesting that individuals follow in my footsteps, nor am I saying that all struggles in life are a curse, I am saying that, in my case, I was spiritually oppressed. Medication was not the solution. The truth of God's Word transformed my life and renewed my mind to peace, joy, and contentment. Today I am a free woman, living in victory because *Christ alone* has set me free. I have been saved, healed, and delivered.

Time and again, as I share my life story, I have been told that it belongs in a book. It is by faith and because of the confirmation of what God placed in my heart as a teenage girl so long ago that I write. For me, writing is being obedient, giving God glory for my life. I am nothing without *Him*.

My life is a testament to the fact that despite whatever this life brings, no matter what was done to you or what you have done to others, through repentance and forgiveness, you can be transformed and live the fullest life Christ died to give you. It is written, "Everyone born of God overcomes the world. This is the victory that has overcome the world, even our faith. Who is it that overcomes the world? Only the one who believes that Jesus is the Son of God" (1 John 5:4–5). *You* can overcome and have true happiness, inner peace, and abundant joy that only God can provide. God's promises are for you too! "Do you want to be made well?" (John 5:6 NKJV).

Most individuals will experience at least one devastating, life-altering event in their lifetimes. As a result, they may doubt God's presence and even lose hope. The purpose of this book is to reach broken people, restore their hope, and encourage them by sharing God's faithfulness through one woman's story of overcoming brokenness and living a peaceful, joy-filled life of victory. Jesus is THE WAY!

Over the years, God has faithfully restored my soul and redeemed my life and the lives of many of my family members. Once we were lost, but now we are found. Once we were cursed, but now we are very much blessed in Christ Jesus. I am His daughter. He loves me and is pleased with the woman I have become. Today, when I look into my eyes, whether in a picture or a mirror, I can see God's promises fulfilled in my reflection. There is no greater joy than looking back at myself and seeing all God has done, knowing apart from Him I could do nothing.

As a God-fearing woman living in obedience to fulfill my God-given destiny, it is my prayer that you will be blessed, encouraged, and inspired as I share my life of brokenness, hope, courage, patience, and perseverance. I pray, too, that God allows you to see *His* hand moving throughout your own life. By His stripes, I have been healed and set free to be me, Tracy Jane Michaud.

God is in control. My life is not my own. *To God be all the glory.*

CHAPTER 1

The Abusive Years

Be still before the Lord
and wait patiently for him;
do not fret when people succeed in their ways,
when they carry out their wicked schemes.

Psalm 37:7

THEY SAY THAT CHILDREN WHO LIVE THROUGH SEXUAL ABUSE HAVE several things in common. For one thing, the perpetrator, or in my case perpetrators, is usually a trusted relative or friend of the family—someone no one would expect, maybe even likeable. They use intimidation, manipulation, and fear tactics to keep the secret, often in the form of threats against the victim or someone the victim loves. I, like many victims of abuse, was taken through a period of grooming that lasted several years. This is the time it takes for the perpetrator to gain the victim's trust, preparing them for what they've been planning all along—sexual molestation, rape, victimization. At least that was how it was for me.

I started out in life with the odds stacked against me, born under a family curse, I guess you could say. When my mother, Debra, was a young child, her parents divorced. My grandmother, Emily, remarried a man who later adopted both my mother and her older brother, who died of a drug overdose years later. By the time my mother was thirteen, my grandmother became very ill and was admitted to Kalamazoo State Hospital as an alcoholic. She received electroshock therapy as part of her inpatient treatment.

Two years later, my grandparents divorced. My grandmother was placed in an adult foster care home, because she was declared mentally incompetent, unable to care for herself or her children. My mother and her brother remained in the home of their stepfather, Ron. Eventually, my grandmother died at the age of fifty-nine from lung cancer. I was twenty-one.

My father immigrated to the United States from the Netherlands as a young boy. He was sixteen and my mother was seventeen when they met in high school. She fell head over heels in love with him. They dated and soon learned a baby was on the way. This changed their relationship significantly. I was conceived in sin, unwanted, just a product of teenage sex. My mother quit attending school during her pregnancy. They were no longer together when my mother gave birth. I was told they tried to work on their relationship, but it just did not work. I don't think my mother ever got over it. She had me, even raised me, but not happily.

According to my mother, at 10:00 p.m., the evening before my birth, she went to the hospital. Six hours later, I took my first breath. I, Tracy Jane, was born into this world in 1972. I was named after my grandmother, Emily Jane, and my mother, Debra Jane—two women far from God, full of insecurity, fear, and regret.

Looking back on who was in my life at that time, I believe I was sustained and upheld by the Lord solely because of my step-grandfather's prayers. From the moment he laid eyes on me, he declared, "It's a miracle." Maybe most of my family members were far from God, but I believe my grandpa Ron knew the Lord a little; having faith the size of a mustard seed is all the faith you need to get started with God. He prayed for my mother and me. The prayers of the righteous availeth much, as the Scripture says.

Setting the Stage

Now a single, teenaged mother who came from a broken home, my mother had her own broken home to manage. She was harsh, selfish, and had a nasty habit of smoking cigarettes. My mother began smoking at the age of eleven—just a little girl—and even smoked throughout her pregnancy with me. With assistance from a couple

24

of relatives, she found an apartment to rent. She had to support the two of us and was forced to grow up fast.

Although my mother provided the basics of food, clothing, and shelter, she did not properly care for me. She lacked the knowledge to attend to my physical needs. My mother was self-focused and enjoyed having many friends over to hang out. I was not her priority. Since I had been exposed to secondhand smoke in utero and from birth, I suffered from many chronic respiratory infections for the first full year of my life. From August to December I was hospitalized for a total of twenty-eight days for things like pneumonia, anemia, scabies, the flu, and respiratory infections. Mind you, this was the seventies, the time before the surgeon general declared secondhand smoke as toxic.[1] This was the beginning of observable neglect and many future hospitalizations.

My mother was a waitress and a cashier, using several babysitters to watch me. She was very wise with what money she earned. She saved and saved. When I was a little over two years old, I began attending Hope Church Nursery School. My mother brought me there wanting the best for me—I realize this full well. I recall naptime at the daycare center being scary for some reason. I was full of fear when it came to lying down—I was too young to understand.

Hope is also where my mother met Ivan, her future husband. She often left me alone in his care while she played Bingo with her girl-friend, Vicki. Concerned, a female relative of my mother approached her directly saying that she must place me, her child, as a priority. My mother disregarded the conversation without any hesitation. I wished she had heeded that warning, then maybe my life would have been very different. The stage was set for the grooming to begin.

As a little girl, I dreaded bedtime because Ivan routinely molested me during prayer time. Imagine that. My first introduction to God and Jesus was made by my predator. Now I know there is a special place in hell for people like that, but as a little girl, and eventually a teenager, how could I have possibly known that? Jesus said, "If anyone causes one of these little ones—those who believe in me—to stumble, it would be better for them to have a large millstone hung around their neck and to be drowned in the depths of the sea. Woe to the world because of the things that cause people to stumble! Such things must come, but woe to the person through whom they come!" (Matthew 18:6–7). My perspective on God and Jesus was warped and twisted for a very long time.

As much as my mother seemed to not care much about me, she *did* keep a baby book for me and would often make notes about my development. She noted a characteristic I had at this age was moodiness and the propensity to sing whenever the radio was on. I do recall music being on a lot. Many songs that I heard back then I have a deep connection with today because of the comfort they gave to me while growing up.

I don't know why Ivan was this way; however, a niece of his told me incest happened in his family. You see, the thing about abusers is that they tend to have been abused themselves. It's part of the whole generational-curse thing that goes on down the family lines until someone has the clarity and courage to break it. I eventually became determined to be that generational-curse breaker—and I was.

My mother and Ivan married in 1976, a couple of years after they met. I was three at the time, and now I had two stepbrothers and a stepsister who moved in with us for a short time but later moved out. I was a child, so I did not know or understand why they left. It was not talked about.

What I did know was that now my predator lived in my home. My stepfather was always trying to touch me, to the point where I grew very picky about my clothes. I needed to have my pants pulled way up, and I always wore long-sleeved shirts. He used to place the end of the vacuum hose on my panties when he was vacuuming. I was habitually molested by my stepfather in our home, the place that was supposed to be safe, secure, and free from fear.

My mother worked and played Bingo, often leaving me home alone with him. When she was gone, I felt sad. She played Bingo frequently, so I felt this way a lot. I was always afraid. I remember the house vividly, as I spent many fearful years there. I particularly remember our basement. My stepfather had made a play area for me and the other little kids who came over. It was very dark, damp, and smelled like newborn puppies. I did not like to go down there, but many times I had no choice.

Still to this day, every time I hear the piano playing in the beginning of the song "Someone Saved My Life Tonight" by Elton John, my whole being is pierced, reminding me of terrible memories lived by that scared little girl down in the basement.

Yet even though there was great tension, constant bickering, and strife in my family, I had a wonderful grandmother on my birth father's side. I would go visit her once in a while, even staying overnight. From the earliest memories with my grandma, I recall happiness and freedom when I was with her. She was a seamstress, always working on something. I enjoyed spending time with my grandma and watching her in the kitchen while she made me authentic Dutch mini-pancakes, called *poffertjes*. They were delicious. Little did she know she was giving me a view of what a normal life looked like, which was far different from the dysfunctional one I was living. God is wonderful that way. Even when the people in your life are far from Him, causing pain, misery, and chaos, there are always those who love Him serving as safe havens and peacemakers and friends. As a little girl, all I knew is that I felt safe with my grandmother. I think she even liked me.

The Yellow-Eyed Monster

Fear was something instilled in me at a very young age. I was always running by the windows in the living room to get to and from my bedroom. It was not until I began gathering and reading through my collection of childhood belongings that I realized exactly where this haunting memory had come from.

When I was two, my mother ordered a "Read About Me Book" titled, *Me and the Yellow-Eyed Monster.* It is a book specifically written to include me, my real-life address, my friends, and my pet. The story is about a scary monster on the loose in Holland, Michigan, where I lived.

Police were called. The detective said, "Monsters always prowl in the dark." Wow, no wonder I was always afraid. Fear is like a dark cloud or lingering shadow that looms over your mind and body, imprisoning you with apprehension of what is to come. It's an uneasiness in your mind that steals your joy and cripples your thoughts. I would often feel my heart beating wildly inside my chest only to realize that at every turn of my head or visual in my mind, there was nothing physically present. I lacked trust in my parents because when I felt scared, alone, or helpless, they disregarded my pleas for help. I was never comforted.

I was especially afraid of my stepfather, as you can imagine. The inappropriate touching continued during the nightly lineup of television shows. He made me promise not to tell anyone and said that if I told my mother, she would not believe me anyway. On my fifth birthday, I woke up saying, "I am bigger now!" For this birthday my mother gave me some Play-Doh, and my stepfather gave me a night light. I think it's ironic that my stepfather bought me a night light. It wasn't the dark I was afraid of; it was him. He would come and tuck me in and say prayers with me and slip his hand under the blanket. Other times he would expose himself to me and have me touch him. I knew at a very young age this was wrong, but I was so scared of him that I just didn't tell.

One day my mother and I met Grandpa Ron at Rivulet Hurst Dairy and Restaurant located near home. My mother told him the doctor had put me on a diet. I was only five years old. I felt ashamed and embarrassed. I remember sneaking food, snacks especially. I had a very unhealthy relationship with food. It just made me feel better somehow. I did not understand why the things were happening to me and why my mother did not protect me. How did she not know? Did she not care? She was my mother!

Music also brought me comfort. Thanks to the one who was abusing me, I knew one thing, and that is that *Jesus loved me.* I still catch myself singing this song. A few other songs and artists that bring me back to this time in my youth are "December, 1963 (Oh, What a Night)" by The Four Seasons, "Disco Duck" by Rick Dees, "Love

Hurts" by Nazareth, and the last one that especially penetrates deeply in my emotions is "Dream Weaver" by Gary Wright. These songs were comforting to me; listening to them over and over again brought me hope that one day I would be fine. Music truly helped me detach from what was happening.

Later that year, I was brought to the hospital and had to have a cystoscopy performed and stay overnight. Nothing more was ever really spoken of why this surgery was necessary. However, in speaking with a dear friend of mine, who is also a registered nurse, she shared that this was a sign of significant abuse.

Dysfunctional Normal

My mother wanted a house to call home for her family, so in 1978 my parents picked out an empty lot in Zeeland, Michigan. They contacted a builder and had a home built from the ground up, everything exactly to their liking. It would not be ready to move into for another year, but they made it happen. That summer, my little sister, Amy, was born. She had reddish-blonde hair and looked like our mother. Although I was five at that time, I learned to change diapers and clothes and assist in many ways. I was excited to help care for my little sister.

During the summer of 1979, my family moved into our new home in Zeeland on West McKinley Avenue. In the fall, I attended first grade at Roosevelt Elementary. Our home was within walking distance, a half mile, so I was considered a "walker." I clearly remember waking myself up by an alarm to get ready for school, because my parents both worked. My sister and I had our own bedrooms. Once I was ready, I would have to wake my one-year-old sister, get her dressed, and bring her to the babysitter a few houses away. I would continue on to school by myself. I often felt sad and alone; however, I loved going to school. After school, I would come home to an empty house and snack while watching television. Eventually, my parents would arrive with my little sister.

I did pretty well in school. My report card had remarks saying, "Excellent effort." However it also read, "Tracy talks too much." Some may say I still do, and that's okay with me. My parents were not involved or interested in anything related to school. I felt unloved and ashamed. Amy and I bounced around from babysitter to babysitter. It was awful.

I met many new friends that year. One friend in particular, Jody, invited me to church. At times, I was allowed to attend. I absolutely loved going. I was so envious of my friend and her family because she lived in a "real family" atmosphere. Behind closed doors in my home environment, I was being abused. While watching television, my stepfather would have me sit behind him on the couch with my legs wrapped around him. He would then reach around and touch my panties. Rarely did my mother join us. One time she stepped into the living room, and I recall my stepfather quickly telling her I was "tickling" him. That was a lie. He was inappropriately touching me. Because he lied to my mother, I knew what he was doing was wrong. I often felt afraid that I may get in trouble from my mother if she saw what he was doing, but she never noticed. I felt yucky, angry, helpless, scared, and so very alone. My stepfather intimidated me, so I listened to him as I always did, and to my mother too.

I went to church with Jody and her family as often as I was allowed. I received my very first Bible as a gift from her mother, Janice. I was seven years old and in the second grade. I treasured my Bible. Although I did not comprehend it, I was fascinated with it. Seeing Jesus' own words in red lettering comforted me. I cannot explain that. I only knew that the Lord loved me and was always with me. I underlined Scripture and wrote in the first page, "Praise Ye the Lord."

I began roller-skating in our basement. I had two pair of roller skates. I had the metal skates which you strapped to the bottom of your shoes. The other pair was Hang Ten name-brand skates. They were my favorite. Oh, they were my pride and joy! I learned how to make pom-poms out of yarn and tied them to the top of the skates.

You see, when I was roller-skating, I would be free, away from my stepfather. We had a stereo downstairs. I would turn the music as loud as I could without getting yelled at and just roller-skate, sing, and dance until I was told otherwise or it was bedtime. I listened to music *all* the time. I was completely enveloped in music. The drums, guitar, piano, the words—all of it just helped me get through each waking day.

Another song that brings me back to this time in my childhood is "The Best of Times" by Styx. These lyrics spoke to me deep in my heart, that one day my mother and I would be close and I would be safe in her arms. "More Than I Can Say" by Leo Sayer made me long for my mother's love. One song that just stopped me in my tracks was a song by Joey Scarbury, the theme song from *The Greatest American Hero*. This song really lifted my spirits.

When Amy wanted to play, we would often play downstairs. My stepfather built a large playhouse for her. It was located in the far corner of the basement. It had room for toys and a few people too. My stepfather would often lure me into it to fondle me when nobody was around. One time my mother came downstairs, and he took off running away from me and pretended to be looking for something. I was scared. I was always scared.

Eventually, on weekends, I began skating at the roller rink. My stepfather would usually drive a friend and me to the skating rink. We stayed one session, sometimes two, depending on what our parents allowed. My friends' parents would take a turn to drop us kids off or pick us up. I was very good at roller-skating. I was incredibly fast too. I won the races many times, which earned me a free drink. My favorite was a frozen cherry cola. When our parents said no and would not take us to the roller rink, we would end up roller-skating in our basement again. All this to say, from the outside, I seemed like a normal young girl; little did anyone know the private hell I was living through.

Our family often drove to visit my stepfather's siblings. He had a large family. A few times I recall my mother coming with, but that seemed rare. The family was very diverse. There were a few families who were established and wealthier than others, while some lived in poverty. Some attended church, while others partied regularly. There were some cousins who attended Christian schools, while others attended public schools. My sister and I had many cousins, older and younger.

I loved all my aunts, uncles, and cousins. I felt freedom playing with my cousins while the parents visited. This was as normal as life could be, considering what was taking place behind closed doors.

To many people, our family was looked upon as "having it all together," and we were considered "well off." Both my parents worked. They owned a home with an in-ground pool. My parents would buy whatever vehicles they were interested in at the moment. Financially, our family was set. However, we didn't vacation or do much for entertainment. Our entertainment was watching recorded movies at home. We watched many movies, and when I say "we," I am referring to my stepfather, my sister, and I. One movie I clearly remember watching was *Porky's*. I recall my stepfather making lewd comments to me while *Porky's* was playing on the VCR. I often ignored him as best I was able without getting punished. This movie was an inappropriate movie for a child my age—or any age, for that matter. However, there were no boundaries, and a moral compass was nonexistent in our home. Amy and I viewed one horror movie after another, such as *Friday the 13th* and *The Exorcist*.

My elementary years were full of daily ups and downs. Attending school, I was excited to be with friends and proud of myself while learning and earning good grades. At home, the abuse continued. My mother was absent a lot, and I was terrorized by my stepfather's constant touching and insistence on being near me. The abuse was progressing. Once my sister was asleep, Ivan would verbally direct me, step-by-step, to do sexual things to him that are appalling.

Ivan's obsession with me grew. He would frequently warn me not to touch another boy, and he would regularly make me feel ashamed of myself. He reminded me over and over again that if I ever told my mother *anything*, that she would not believe me. I was very afraid of him. He knew how to manipulate and scare me. I started to resent him and could not stand to be around him. I hated him. But, as odd as it sounds, I can admit that I loved him too. He was the only father

I knew. My life was total dysfunction. I was a child and knew my life was not normal, but one day it would be okay. I did not understand how; I just knew one day my life would be all right.

While elementary school had always been a safe zone for me, a place where I felt valued, middle school was different. Although I enjoyed "going" to school, I did not have peace while there. I felt rejected. The rejection at home spilled over into my life at school. I lacked joy and confidence. I was not interested in learning anymore. My focus changed from learning to socializing and searching out acceptance, as most middle-school-age children do. My life was full of fear. The abuse continued.

I looked for ways to be busy and to earn money. For a period of time, I walked a little girl to school for a quarter a day. I mowed lawns and began babysitting regularly for my sister's friend and her siblings. Many times I watched the kids overnight and occasionally for an entire weekend. I loved the freedom! I was given money to take the kids to get ice cream, too, and I could also earn extra money by doing the laundry, dishes, vacuuming, and dusting. I truly enjoyed the motherly role in the safety of the couple's home.

I began going to a "fat doctor" with the woman for whom I babysat. My weight fluctuated, often hovering in the 160s. I was considered overweight for my age and height. We went monthly to get weighed. The physician prescribed diet pills, thyroid pills, and a vitamin B shot. I was encouraged by the thought of losing weight and getting in shape.

I will never forget the day when my stepfather came into the living room while I was listening to one of my records. He picked up the record sleeve and pointed out the record label, "Virgin." He then explained to me in graphic detail parts of the female anatomy, and then threatened me saying, "You better be a virgin!"

My life continued in chaotic dysfunction, and my school work suffered. I was having difficulties in English, mostly because I was not able to concentrate. I was present in class, but my mind was always wandering. My mother would often send my stepfather into my bedroom to help me, but help is not what I received. While at school, I began cheating on daily assignments. A few students regularly allowed me to copy their papers, so I did.

I do have some fond memories with my mother at the kitchen table. On occasion, although she was accompanied by a plume of smoke, lit cigarette in hand, and ashtray, she and I would play the board game Scrabble and also compete against each other doing word searches. It was the quality time she spent with me that I cherished the most as a child. Sometimes as a family we played board games, but even that caused tension. Specifically, while playing a game called Life, I was verbally threatened by my stepfather in regard to boys. It became so intense that we did not finish.

The threats gradually increased, and I feared being home. I began to "live to survive" and long for the weekends, whatever the weekend entailed: having a friend overnight, visiting my stepfather's family, roller-skating, or babysitting. Whatever the activity I could get involved in, I was game, as long as I could get away from him and not have to be home alone without my mother.

As I got older, my interest grew in finding out more about my biological father. I periodically asked my mother about my "real dad." Ivan was completely against the idea of me ever going to his home. I would often hear negative remarks to make me rethink wanting to get to know him. At my nagging request, I was able to finally spend some time with my biological father and his family. It was clearly not a living environment I was used to. My parents were clean freaks. Growing up, as a family we deep-cleaned the house often. Every room was detailed from top to bottom. Each room was emptied of dirty clothes, linen, and trash. We dusted, vacuumed, and wiped clean any visible smudge. We cleaned every possible surface that was cleanable, using toothbrushes and toothpicks to get to the nooks and crannies that were unreachable otherwise; this included our parents' vehicles, inside and out. My biological father had several dogs and cats, which basically took over the living space. It smelled horrific. Dirty dishes and clothes were scattered everywhere. I was not impressed; however, I was grateful for the opportunity to see for myself and spend time with him. This did not sit well with my stepfather. His intimidation and threats increased because he wanted me all to himself.

Lies and Betrayal

After ten years of dealing with my stepfather's abuse, something in me snapped. I had finally built up enough courage to tell my mother what he was doing to me. I had a sense of relief. In front of my mother's female friend, I told her how he had been touching me sexually and had for years. Ivan was right. She *did not* believe me, and more so, she began to hate me and called me a liar. I was extremely confused and scared.

To her credit, my mother confronted Ivan, who lied about all of it, and from then on, they both began to treat me differently. "Liar" became one of the many names they called me. I also heard the names "bitch" and "whore," and my little sister would chime in calling me a "fat pig." After my mother told him that I was accusing him of molesting me, my stepfather threatened me and emotionally abused me to the point that I later told them I changed my mind. I denied it. Just as my stepfather always reminded me, my mother did not believe me. I experienced complete betrayal, a defining moment in my life. From that point on, I knew I had to be self-sufficient and self-reliant. I always did what they asked of me because I was afraid. I was determined to just get through each day because my parents were not going to protect me.

I think it's interesting that my stepfather treated me differently around my mother. When she was around, he was verbally abusive and put me down. But when she wasn't home, he was pleading with me not to tell anyone what he was doing to me. He taught me how to drive a car as a way to bribe me to keep quiet. I was only twelve years old, and I felt excited and proud that he trusted me enough to teach me how to operate a manual stick shift and drive his brand-new car. The abuse continued.

I was determined to begin making changes as a way to regain some control over my life. I knew I couldn't control what they did, like cigarette smoking, the abuse, and things like that, but I could do some things for myself. I really began to focus on my health. I started to exercise and watched what I ate. I did not have a clue of how to go about a new lifestyle, so I did the best I could. My stepfather noticed. He would make sexual comments about my body and compare me to women on television. I was disgusted.

Yet somewhere along the way, I started to gain some confidence, the kind of confidence in life that *only* God can provide amidst the circumstances in which I lived. I loved who I was becoming. I knew one day my life was going to be different. When I had a family of my own, life would be extraordinary. I was going to do things better and be an involved parent. *Nobody* was going to abuse my children.

Shortly after I started the eighth grade, Ivan reconnected with his children. He picked them up and drove them back to our home to visit. My parents owned a Singing Machine, a home karaoke device that we would sing along to and record the songs. In fact, I still have the recorded cassette tapes of the singing sessions with my stepsiblings. I enjoyed the time we spent getting to know each other.

It was during this same period of time when Amy and I learned our mother was having an affair with a coworker, whom she later married. It was made known to us after my stepfather had a physical altercation with the man in a parking lot near our home. My parents argued a lot, escalating even to the point of my stepfather punching my mother in her face and head. I had never witnessed physical abuse between them. I was so frightened that I ran to a neighbor's house, and the police were called. Our home was dysfunctional and falling apart. My mother and stepfather announced their separation, and he moved out. Initially, it was all right. But *every weekend* my sister and I had to go with him.

Once Ivan was living in his own apartment, located in Holland, Amy and I began riding along on the weekend pickups and drop-offs of his older children. They lived in Bloomingdale, an hour's drive away. It was a fun time. The radio was always on, whether a cassette tape was playing or whatever stations us kids chose. Music was part of our travel time. We sang and bounced around the car like, well, like the happy kids we were *together*. I am forever grateful for those times of getting to just be goofy and have fun.

One weekend visit to Bloomingdale, I met the Michaud twins, Robert and Albert. They are identical twins, born five minutes apart. The twins were friends of my stepsiblings. This particular day, my stepfather and we arrived, and his children were not ready. We were invited inside to wait. I followed my stepsister down the hallway. She opened the back door to inform her brother we were there waiting. As I stood next to her, Albert noticed me. He told me later, "It was that precise moment in time, I knew one day you would be my wife." Although he did not tell anyone at that time, he was certain; he just knew in his heart that I was the one.

The twins were cute. They had recently turned fifteen years old. I learned that Albert was sexually active, which did not interest me in the least. Robert was not sexually active, which made me like him all the more. One thing that has always remained in my mind from the moment I met them was that one twin wore corduroys and the other Levi's.

Soon after meeting, Robert and I began dating. It was innocent, hand holding, kissing, and a lot of writing letters back and forth during the week. My stepfather found out and threatened me, "You better not have sex with him!" I told him I was not planning to.

I do not recall how it came about, but one weekend I stayed with my stepsiblings. We ended up staying overnight at the twins' house. Their parents were inviting, kind, and did not mind that all of us teenagers were over. And when it came to sleeping arrangements, the boys and girls were separated. Upon saying our goodnights to one another, Albert and I passed each other slowly in the doorway. Out of nowhere, I said to him, "I love you." I do not know where that came from or why I said it. I was dating his twin. The boys slept in the bedroom and the girls on the living room floor. I will never forget the green carpet we lay on. It was old, like their dad. When my stepfather learned of this evening, he again told me that I better not have sex. And once more,

I told him I was not planning to. He was acting a little stranger than normal, but then again, I always thought he was strange.

Robert and I only dated for a short time because my stepfather made me break up with him.

Making Me His

It was New Year's Eve, and my stepfather was going out to celebrate, so he allowed me to spend the night with my stepsiblings at their trailer. The twins were also there, and no parents were present. I was happy to be there with them, but I also felt very uncomfortable, thinking my stepfather may be lurking around outside. We played games and behaved like teens who do not have parental guidance. We rang in the New Year with hugs and kisses. The twins' dad picked them up shortly after that.

Morning arrived. My stepfather came to pick me up. He glared at me, giving intimidating looks and the cold shoulder. He was behaving as if I were his girlfriend who had been flirting with another man. He did not trust me around boys.

Convinced that I was only getting in shape because I was looking to have sex with someone, he watched my every move and frequently made sexual comments. I began eating excessively so I'd be unattractive to him. I hated being his "eye candy." He wanted me to himself and told me this often.

One particular day, not long before we stopped visiting my stepsiblings, Ivan also permitted his oldest daughter, while underage, to drive his car. He was a passenger. Amy and I sat in the back seat while Albert and I secretly held hands. Afterward, for whatever reason, Albert began the mile walk home. Before heading home ourselves, Ivan offered one of his sons and Robert a ride to the Michaud residence. As we approached the front yard, he slid the car sideways on the gravel road. Once the boys were out of the car, Ivan turned to me and said, "If you ever date Albert, I will hang him by his balls in the rafters of the barn across the street from his house." He then declared, "We are not going to Bloomingdale anymore."

My stepfather's behavior toward me was extremely controlling and possessive. Once, when his weekend visit was over, he dropped my sister and me back off to our mother's home and insisted that she not allow me to make long-distance phone calls. She agreed to his face, but she allowed me to anyway. Secretly, over the phone, Albert and I started dating. Once again, my stepfather learned that I was dating and once more threatened me about having sex. He made me break up with Albert also, as he was certain that I was going to have sex with him. Kids and crushes, that's all it was, nothing more, or so I thought at the time.

Eventually, my stepfather began having me watch pornography with him while visiting him at his apartment. Amy was not there, nor do I know where she was during these times. During the weekdays, my mother was never around. She worked hard, and when she had free time, mostly every night of the week, you could find her at the local Bingo hall with a cigarette in her mouth. Many weeknights Ivan would pick us girls up and bring us home later in the evening. His behavior only grew more bizarre.

During another weekend visit, my stepfather threatened to take Amy and me down south, so he could marry me. I was so afraid. I was scared to death of him, and I hated him and did not want him touching me. I certainly did not want to marry him! I did not want to be around him at all. One time he actually drove my sister and me toward Indiana, and with a lot of screaming and crying, we convinced him not to take us away. We ended up staying overnight at his parents' apartment in Fennville, Michigan.

Later in the weekend, he gave me his wedding ring. Without arguing, I took it and put it on my thumb. When he dropped us off at my mother's home, my mother noticed the ring. As I walked through the back door, she tackled me to get it. She was enraged. I gave it to her. It didn't mean anything to me. *I did not want it!* I only took it so he would stop begging me. I just didn't want him to try and marry me down south, so I took it home. Not only was I afraid of my stepfather, at this point, I was afraid of my mother too.

I begged my mother to let me stay home and not make me go to my stepfather's apartment during spring break. The day came when Ivan arrived, and although she told him that I did not want to go with him, she still made me go. He was furious! He was not happy with me at all.

Ivan lived upstairs in a very small one-bedroom apartment. One night he was out late partying, so Amy and I went to bed. She went to sleep in his bedroom, as she always did, and I was lying on the living room floor. As the door opened, he came stumbling in, vibrating the floor, and making a lot of noise. Although I was awakened by the commotion, the second I heard him, I pretended to be asleep.

I don't know if he checked in on my sister or not because I had my head covered. He approached the living room. I did not see him, but the sound of his footsteps made me aware of his presence. He then moved the blanket and pulled up my knee-length nightshirt. I couldn't move. I was paralyzed with fear. I realized that this was it; this was the night he was actually going to "stick it in," as he was *always* saying, which had made me afraid to go to sleep whenever I was with him.

It happened so fast. My eight-year-old sister was there. Amy witnessed her father rape me, though she did not disclose this information for several decades. I was only fourteen years old. I laid there with tears dripping down my face, not really knowing what to do next. Do I get up? Then he would know that I was awake. Or should I just lie there? It didn't take long for a decision to be made. He made it for me. "Get up and go douche," he commanded. "It is behind the toilet with instructions."

Hours later, after crying and showering, I came out of the bathroom. My stepfather then announced I was no longer a virgin. That was a change-moment in my life. It set a label upon me, and an identity I didn't want. I truly believe it set me on a course of self-reliance and destructive behavior. I had an internal dialogue that screamed around the clock, "You are unlovable," "You are damaged," "You are worthless." I was deeply wounded, completely shattered, insecure, and rejected. I was "used goods," in my view. The shame that attached to my soul was as present as my heartbeat. A constant reminder of my reality.

My stepfather constantly begged me to marry him so he wouldn't get into trouble if I ever told on him. A few weeks went by, and he began threatening that if I ever told anybody, he would kill me. He said there was no way I was putting him in jail and that he would kill us both first.

Everything, and I mean *my whole world*, was changed, and changing by the minute! I was so confused and lost. The tape played over and over in my head, *"If you ever tell anybody, I will kill you,"* and *"I am not going to jail; I will kill us both first."* I was scared because I truly believed him! Words cannot express how terrified I was.

Soon after, I went to school and asked to see our school counselor. I was determined to tell *everything*. After all, what did I have to lose? I had nobody but myself anyway. If I died, I died. I attempted to tell my best friend during shop class, but as soon as she said she wouldn't want to be friends with someone who had sex, I clammed up. I couldn't lose her too. When I arrived for my appointment with the counselor, I turned the corner, and there stood Ivan. He did not know that I was there to see the counselor. He signed me out, and as we walked to the car, he told me again that he would kill me if I ever told anybody. I got into the car and was silent, speechless, and afraid. I sat very still in the passenger seat. I did not understand. Why was he here? He was supposed to be at work. Ivan drove to Holland. He promised to buy me a car, a gold Fiero, if I kept my mouth shut. I agreed.

My stepfather then drove me to his apartment. He pulled quickly into his garage and closed the door because family lived nearby. He instructed me to rush up the stairs and open the white built-in cabinet with glass doors. Inside were many condoms. Well, I knew what those were for. I groaned inwardly, depressed and helpless. My stepfather sent me into his bedroom to remove my clothing. Then someone knocked at the door. He had me hide behind clothing and a vacuum, completely naked. I was so relieved and yet scared to death all at the same time. Who was it? Did he think I turned him in? Was it my mother? The police? What I wouldn't give to have someone of authority at the door.

It was one of his nephews. They were out in the dining area, laughing. I don't know if his nephew knew I was in the bedroom or not, but when he left, Ivan entered the bedroom. I stayed tucked away until he yelled at me to come out. My mind was made up. *Somehow, someway, somebody* had to believe me. This had to stop!

I wasn't sure I knew who I was anymore. As a young girl, the molestation brought about daily shame. Now, I lost my sense of self-worth. I felt dirty. I became insecure, and an unshakable dark cloud followed. I thought about running away, but where would I go? I thought about my biological father, but that's about it. My mother did not believe me two years previously, so I definitely was not going to tell her Ivan had raped me and was now threatening my life!

I *always* enjoyed going to school . . . not anymore. My focus was not there. I began skipping. Even though my stepfather lived in another city, he knew each time when I was staying home. My step-father repeatedly raped me. Although he never used abusive physical measures, he had groomed me, instilling fear at a very young age and regularly reminding me that my mother would not believe me. Through his manipulating threats and the power he had over me as my parent, the abuse continued.

My only hope at that time was to get the car he had promised me and to drive south until I ran out of gas somewhere. Not much of a plan at fourteen, but it was my coping mechanism for the dysfunctional reality in which I lived.

Everything in me wanted to make my life safe and happy with my little sister. I made a promise to myself that I was *never* going to allow another person to hurt me. When I had children, I was always going to love and protect them above all else, being the best mother possible. When I was home alone, I loved to sing and dance. I did a lot of eating and crying too. Day after day, I begged my mother to let me stay home on the weekends. Each time she answered with an emphatic "NO!"

CHAPTER 2

Poor Choices

But you, God, see the trouble of the afflicted;
you consider their grief and take it in hand.
The victims commit themselves to you;
you are the helper of the fatherless.

Psalm 10:14

JUNE 13, 1987, WAS A DAY I'LL NEVER FORGET. SCHOOL WAS OUT for the summer, and it was Saturday, the day when my sister and I had to go stay with my stepfather, a man I hated. For weeks, I had begged and pleaded with my mother to allow me to stay home and not make me go with him. I even promised to do whatever she asked, to clean whatever she needed, take care of Amy, and I would stay out of her way as long as she did not make me go. My mother told me she would think about it. However, the weekend had arrived, and I still did not have an answer.

My stepfather was pulling into our driveway. I couldn't bear to think that during this time I may have to be alone with him. I felt my body trembling inside. He disgusted me. Everything about his appearance just sickened me. Ivan was tall and slim. He was very feminine and always reeked of stale smoke. He frequently wore tank top shirts and short cut-off jean shorts, with white material from the bottom of his pockets exposed. He had a large distinctive nose and wore glasses that tinted when outdoors. I was repulsed by him. That day, I specifically recall our kitchen window being wide open. That deeply concerned me because of the possibility of him hearing me ask my mother again if I could stay home, but I asked her anyway. I will never forget how helpless I felt when at the top of her voice, she yelled at me saying, "You are going, and don't be driving!" I shuddered.

Ivan sauntered into the house, giving me a threatening look. I knew I was in trouble just by how he glared at me. Amy and I gathered our belongings, carried them to the car, and went with him. We had no choice. He had me sit in the back seat, which was unusual. I knew he had overheard my mom. He was constantly glaring at me through the rearview mirror. A sense of dread flooded my mind.

It was a warm day. We drove with the windows down. As he headed out of town, taking all the back roads, we drove in complete silence. Normally, the radio was on, but this day was different. His behavior was abnormal. I believed that he was "punishing" me by having me sit in the back of the car and not allowing the radio to be on because he overheard my request.

Upon approaching his nephew's home, he began acting more strangely. My stepfather appeared emotional, uncertain, and flustered about something. I did not feel safe.

Ivan's demeanor had changed over the past few months. Growing up I had never witnessed him drinking, but now he was openly drinking alcohol and smoking marijuana and cigarettes in front of us girls and our friends. At times, he insisted and pressured me to smoke the marijuana with him, teaching me how to roll a joint. Ivan also purchased alcohol for my friends and me and encouraged us to drink when he watched us girls overnight at his apartment.

That day he was acting very weird. I am unclear on the exact order of events or how long we stayed, but when it was time to leave, a family friend, who I will call Sara and who was a year younger than me, came along. I was happy. I didn't know her all that well, but I liked her and I was glad she was coming with us. Her presence was comforting, since I would not have to be alone with my stepfather if my sister left.

Apparently, Amy was staying at her friend's house for the evening. I don't think she knew because when my stepfather told her to get out of the car, she started crying. Amy stood in the driveway frantically screaming and crying, and in the loudest voice you can imagine an eight-year-old girl could yell, she bellowed out, *"I hate you, Ivan. I wish you would die!"* Little did she know those would come to be the last words she would ever speak to her father.

As he backed out of the driveway and left my sister bawling, he mentioned that we were going to a graduation party. Thirty minutes later we arrived at another family member's home. We pulled into the driveway. Ivan got out of the car and walked up to the house. Sara and I waited in the car. Nobody was home. My stepfather got back in the car, flopped his head back toward the headrest, and closed his eyes. He was high, and I was scared. I said, "I can drive." Without hesitation, we changed seats, put our seat belts on, and proceeded down the road.

I was very familiar with this area, as my stepfather often drove around out in the country. He kept a bottle opener in the little compartment above the stick shift because he frequently purchased bottled pop for us along the way. Little did I know that four-inch piece of metal would forever alter my life. I took the route we had driven many times. On a few occasions, Ivan drove Amy and I down this road just for the way it made your stomach turn. It felt like you were on a roller coaster. The road was covered in gravel and had a very steep hill on it. I continued onto 54th Street northbound, going approximately fifty-five miles per hour.

Once we arrived on the other side of the hill, we collectively decided to turn around and go back down the hill. My stepfather said we had time because he wasn't planning to be at the party until 6:00 p.m. The second time down the hill, my stepfather encouraged me to go faster, so I did.

I accelerated along a stretch of road that had loose gravel leading to the crest of the hill, and we were going so fast that the trees looked like a blur. I came over the hill and felt the car lift off the road. I had no traction. The car began sliding and rotating counterclockwise. I begged for my stepfather's help. All I remember was him laughing.

It all happened so fast. I lost complete control of the car as we skidded over 175 feet, downhill; the car rolled over and landed on the driver's side. We had hit a tree on the opposite side of the road going eighty-five miles per hour.

The front end of the car—from the driver's side to the passenger's side, across the dash and front-seat compartment area—was fully wrapped around the tree, suspended in the air. While the undercarriage of the car faced the road, the back of the car still rested on the graveled edge.

Then there was *complete* silence. All I could hear was myself breathing. I was trapped. I felt absolutely *no physical pain*. I was pinned in the car. My face was pressed up against the driver's pillar with my abdomen on the northside of the tree, while my legs were around the southside of the tree. I was wrapped completely in metal and car parts.

It was dreamlike. My thoughts turned to my mother. Truly, the only thing that had me worried at this tragic moment was my mother finding out that I didn't listen to her. She knew when I was with my stepfather that he allowed me to drive, but this particular day *was the only time* she ever told me not to drive. All I ever wanted from my mother was her approval. She was going to be so disappointed in me.

I was distressed. I couldn't move. My stepfather did not answer me when I talked to him. He had taken the brunt of the impact. His face was dark purple; his upper body was crushed with metal car body components. His legs were wedged between the floorboard of the car and the tree itself. I was pretty sure he was dead but thought maybe he was just unconscious.

I began to scream for help, but the only response was Sara screaming too. She was laying on the ground directly beneath me in the gully. Her leg was broken and bleeding excessively. I began to panic when I realized we were in the middle of nowhere, out in the country. No matter how loud we screamed, we would not be heard.

I am uncertain about how much time passed as we yelled and screamed for someone to hear us. From the police report and witness account, it had been approximately three hours before help arrived. A passerby noticed skid marks on the opposite side of the hill as he drove, and he stopped when he observed the traumatic scene at the bottom. He quickly realized that he needed to go call for help, because there were no cell phones readily available back then. I am forever grateful for that man since his actions saved my life.

When the Allegan County police, Hamilton Fire Department, and Mercy Ambulance arrived, I was fully alert, communicating, and able to answer questions. However, shortly after, my hearing sense took over. I personally would compare this "feeling" to the experience of having an anesthesiologist administer medication before a surgical procedure, which causes the voices of all who are near to be magnified. There was a brief time of confusion and helplessness. I was having difficulty breathing, gasping for air, when suddenly the sergeant from the Allegan County sheriff's department lifted my head, which opened my airway, and I began breathing freely once again.

Sara sustained a badly broken leg and was taken by ambulance to the nearest hospital. It's a miracle she survived, having been thrown from the car. Sara was not wearing a seat belt. She was sitting in the middle of the back seat, leaning forward with her elbows resting on the front bucket seats, watching as I sped down the road. I reconnected with her several years later, sharing a meal, but that was the extent of our friendship.

I vaguely recall a voice coming from behind me. I was comforted by the presence of help, but I was critically injured. Chaos was going on around me. I heard multiple people speaking loud and fast. I heard words like "hypotension," "shock," and "significant lower extremity trauma." I was confused because I didn't feel any pain. There was a lot of commotion and discussion about how to get me out of the car without causing additional injuries.

At that time, Butterworth Hospital, located in Grand Rapids, Michigan, was the area's only level-one trauma center. Emergency records stated that a trauma team was awaiting my arrival with "no ETOA" (estimated time of arrival) because there was a "long extraction time." For over an hour, a hydraulic apparatus called the Jaws of Life was used to pry apart the car. The constant running and straining of the engine, and the screeching and creaking of metal from the groaning car are haunting sounds forever etched into my memory.

I faintly heard someone tell me they were going to get me out of the car and to keep my eyes closed. I could hear a helicopter in the distance. It was coming closer and getting louder. My thoughts turned again to my mother. She was really going to be disappointed with me.

Aero Med helicopter landed nearby, and immediately, the flight physician and nurse who specialized in trauma emergency and critical care began working with the emergency medical technicians (EMTs) who were on scene.

It was mass confusion for me. The excessive talking from so many people impaired my comprehension. I was being talked to continuously. I specifically remember hearing, "Stay with me, Tracy." I heard that several times.

Once my broken, bloody body was freed from the wreckage, my lower body was placed in military antishock pants to prevent bleeding to death. I was resuscitated and then carried up the hill for transport by helicopter.

The noise of the helicopter, the sound of the dispatch-radio voices, and the sensation of lifting off the ground while lying on the stretcher are unforgettable. Although the helicopter was loud, I was continuously being talked to during the flight. To this day, I can recognize the vibrations in the air of a medical helicopter in the distance. As it flies overhead, many emotions are evoked within me. I immediately pray for the medically unstable individual for whom it has been dispatched, as well as their family.

When we landed at the hospital, I was rushed into the emergency room where I was surrounded by complete chaos. I wasn't sure where my stepfather was at that time. Was he here in the hospital too? Was he okay? I began having nightmares of him coming to the hospital to kill me, while I pulled out IVs to get away from him. I was terror-stricken when I realized the severity of my situation, plus nobody was forthcoming with any information about him.

Ivan was proud of each car he owned. From the Corvette to the Chevette and every vehicle in between, he took great care of his cars, detailing and cleaning them often, then driving to family members' homes, boasting of his precious idols. I thought about how irate he was going to be that his car was damaged. I knew I would pay.

Once I learned that my stepfather was actually dead, I was distraught. On one hand, I felt an overwhelming sense of relief because he was no longer going to hurt me. On the other hand, I felt a deep sadness, and at times cried uncontrollably. I was thoroughly broken. I did not feel guilty because I fully understood that it was an accident, but I felt a deep sorrow for my stepfather. The only father figure I knew had died while I was behind the wheel driving.

I knew in my heart that God had saved me, but nobody offered any information about my situation. What was wrong with my body? Would I live or die from my injuries? I really had no idea what I was up against. If I had, I probably would have given up.

CHAPTER 3

Surviving and Determined

Do not fear [anything], for I am with you;
Do not be afraid, for I am your God.
I will strengthen you, be assured I will help you;
I will certainly take hold of you with My righteous right hand
[a hand of justice, of power, of victory, of salvation].

Isaiah 41:10 (AMP)

IN THE EMERGENCY ROOM AT BUTTERWORTH HOSPITAL, DOCTORS, nurses, technicians, interns, and other staff gathered around me without delay. The chaos that ensued left me feeling helpless. The ER physician led the trauma team. He requested several consultations and physical examinations.

The room was full of activity. I was alert and continuously being talked to and asked questions; specifically, I recall being asked if I wore glasses or contacts. I answered that I did, and soon after that, someone was standing next to me who told me to open my eyes wide while they removed each contact lens. I did not like that, since I was unable to see *anything* clearly. I communicated to the best of my ability as I was being poked and prodded.

The list of injuries was long. I heard words like "massive trauma," "blood loss," and "multiple fractures." All kinds of doctors were present, each performing their own consult examinations, such as orthopedic, cardiac, plastic surgeons, pediatricians, anesthesiologists, vascular docs, and others.

Evaluation in the emergency room revealed that I was "mildly hypotensive" with "severe massive soft tissue wounds to both thighs."

I was placed on oxygen, several IVs were put into my veins in both arms, many X-rays were taken, and a catheter was inserted into my bladder since I would not be using the restroom independently for months.

Although I denied having chest pain, shortness of breath, or abdominal pain, at this point, *I was experiencing pain*. However, I was informed that I could not have pain medication until further tests were performed. Little did I know that the physical pain I was feeling in that moment would be nothing in comparison to what I was about to endure throughout my life. Even though I was only a teenager, I would become very familiar with medical terminology. I would learn to take my own blood pressure and pulse, even becoming my own advocate. I had no idea of what was to come.

I am only able to provide details from my hospitalization because of the information taken directly from my medical records. Without being able to see clearly, and with the unfamiliar voices and commotion—not to mention the absence of my mother and stepfather—the details at the time were confusing. I remember being scared but calm, knowing that I was in the care of professionals and believed I would be safe.

After two hours of my body being attended to, the trauma team realized that I was unable to move my right leg, having no sensation, and my foot had no pulse, meaning the blood flow was cut off and my leg was dying. I was taken immediately to the operating room.

The orthopedic surgeon and his assistant operated on my leg, along with a number of specialists, including a vascular surgeon. Even though they were aware of the situation with my right foot, they began on my left thigh, but not before they intubated me. I was now on life support. After an hour, the bleeding was controlled. Both legs were extremely contaminated with compound fractures to the femurs, leaving bone and marrow exposed. Another three hours passed as the team cleaned the massive wounds from "flecks of car body," "hair," "paint," and "dirt." Then the dead tissue was removed, and my wounds were sterilized once more. Finally, after removing Ivan's four-inch bottle opener, which had been embedded into my right femoral artery, my leg was repaired. My right foot redeveloped a pulse and regained color. Both legs had pins inserted for traction, and my pelvis was placed in a sling. I was transferred to the surgical intensive care unit with a "guarded prognosis" and required close care as the physicians expected pneumonia to develop.

The trauma team diligently worked for over six hours to sustain my life. In addition to broken leg bones and pelvic bones, I also had broken bones in my right hand and wrist.

Within just the first forty-eight hours after the car accident, my entire body was replaced with blood seven times over.

Amputated, but Alive

I wasn't out of the woods yet. On several occasions, I was taken to the operating room to re-debride, to cut out and remove dead tissue to freshen up the wounds from both thighs. That was agonizing, torturous pain. The blunt force that was used deep inside my legs to scrape around my femur was nauseating. My legs still have deep aches of pain to this day. I was also seen by the plastic surgery department, and they evaluated and helped with the debriding of the thighs as well. They were having trouble with bleeding from vein grafts that failed, and my lungs wouldn't fully expand. I had several episodes of hypotension but responded well with fluids, blood, and dopamine. The team of specialists were especially worried about my legs as the tissues continued to die even while on a wide variety of antibiotics. It went on like this over the next week. Everything went from bad to worse. Although my body was lined with ice-packed bags and continuously pumped full of antibiotics, my fever had approached 107 degrees due to gangrene and septic shock setting in.

I hazily recall hearing people talking near my bedside about amputation. I heard a man's voice say, "You are very sick. We need to amputate your leg or you will die." I clearly remember saying that I didn't want to die; however, I am uncertain if I mouthed those words or if I only thought those words in reaction. Without a doubt, I did not want to die.

I cannot describe the deep sadness that I feel when I read what was done to me. As I write, I am literally experiencing phantom pain and wiping tears for the broken little girl who had to endure so much for a chance to live. A life forever altered.

Although I knew that my leg had been surgically removed, it wasn't visibly evident when I lifted my head and looked down, due to the large bandages that wrapped my thigh. I still felt it; there was pain and my toes constantly tingled. It didn't feel amputated. What I didn't understand until later is that the nerve endings are still alive and that I would forever "feel" my leg, or parts of it, even experiencing intense phantom pain.

I vividly recall the first time I actually "noticed" my leg was gone. That day I saw my leg without bandages. I was in a tub of water, a Hubbard tank, and I was fully immersed while the doctors began to clean the inside of my legs. I was horrified; all I saw was muscle and bone. I freaked out. I was traumatized to say the least and began pulling IVs out, trying to get off the chain-link stretcher that had lowered me into the tank. They quickly drugged me, and I woke up later in my room.

A few days after the amputation, I was taken back to the operating room to clean out the stump with Betadine and peroxide. *Stump* is one of the terms used to refer to an amputated limb. I prefer *residual limb*, but either one is correct. My physician hand-packed sterile gauze, placing it inside my thigh region to fill in where muscle had been, but had to leave the end of my stump partially open due to the infection and need for daily scrubbing, so my femur was exposed. I had so much flesh ripped off my body during the extraction from the car that the remaining tissues had to heal from the bone outward. It was a slow and lengthy healing process. I was told that once my body was fully healed, I would be fitted with a prosthesis, an artificial leg. I accepted that, but I had no idea at the time how very complicated my situation would be.

Critical Care, Excruciating Pain

Being in the critical care unit was so isolating. My vague recollection of that time is filled with beeping machines, respiratory therapists, nurses, doctors, and interns who gathered around my bedside frequently while discussing one area of concern at a time. I had intense, excruciating pain throughout my body, but mostly from my pelvis area and lower extremities. My thoughts screamed, but no one could hear me. I often gave way to the morphine and slept.

Eventually, I developed pneumonia. My left lung collapsed, and the right lung was following suit. I had to have breathing treatments to assist in healing. It was frightening. I am forever thankful for those treatments, but at the time, it angered me each time they approached me.

Day after day, several times daily, I would return to the operating room to have pain inflicted upon me. I hated every minute of knowing that I had to endure this to give myself a chance to heal a little further. My legs were unpacked from the previous gauze, all dead tissue removed with a scalpel and scissors, then wounds cleaned and scrubbed with Betadine. Once the sterile solution was used to completely clean the wounds, my legs were repacked one Kerlix gauze roll at a time. I would return to my room in the surgical intensive care unit.

My days and nights were indistinguishable. I was attached to a machine that dripped morphine into my vein automatically to keep pain bearable. In the first days, while intubated, I was able to communicate to others through blinking. My right arm was casted. Although I am dominantly right-handed, I was also able to use my left hand to write to others when assisted by another in holding the pad of paper. Many times it was not readable. It was frustrating when individuals would try to make out my scribbles, and I could not express my message clearly because I was so heavily sedated.

There were so many different medical procedures that I had to suffer through. I had to have a thoracentesis performed to remove excess fluid buildup between my lungs and chest wall. My doctor made an incision in my rib cage and pushed a tube into my lung lining to relieve the pressure and pain. At one point my heart became enlarged, and I was sent for an ECG and treated. Again, I began experiencing deep pain in my right side; after more testing, my gallbladder was removed. Due to the extensive portion of dead femur, I had to undergo a bone autograft. The surgeons removed bone from my left hip and transplanted it into my left thigh to stimulate the growth of new femur bone. It took some time, but it was successful.

Among the daily procedures, several times a day, I was given Versed. Versed is a medication given to produce short-term amnesia for a select period of time where *excruciating pain is involved*. When the medication wears off, it allows the patient to "forget" the experience. However, there were a few times I wasn't given enough medication, and I freaked out during dressing changes. It was awful.

I was under anesthesia more times than I can list for procedures to insert pins into my bones and later remove them; to have my left knee and ankle manipulated to retain range of motion; and to remove bone spurs and calcium deposits from my stump, and for various other treatments. I endured over thirty surgeries, with a few more plastic surgery revisions after I was discharged. That is too many surgeries for anyone, let alone a fourteen-year-old.

From the moment of arrival and admission, respiratory therapists closely monitored my breathing, treating my pulmonary function. Although the process was extremely demanding, and the suctioning frightened me every time, I am grateful for each individual who assisted in keeping my lungs properly functioning. I never, ever take breathing for granted. Every breath is a gift.

I also had to face multiple skin grafts to repair my mangled thighs. The head plastic surgeon and his team, among many others, assisted in harvesting 25 percent of my body surface. They removed healthy skin from both of my lower extremities and stitched it into place over my thigh wounds. This was an excruciating process. Only those who have endured this will fully understand the physical pain involved. From the time of the car accident throughout my treatment, my entire body was replaced with blood over ten times.

Visitors

Due to the constant drip of pain medication, I am unable to recall who may have come to the hospital to visit while I was in the intensive critical care unit or even the surgical intensive care unit. I was told that due to the severity of my situation, only limited immediate family was allowed and only briefly. I barely remember my mother and best friend standing near my bed. But it had to have been close to six weeks before I actually recalled familiar faces. Once I was placed in the pediatric unit, I was aware of who visited. I knew many medical personnel gathered at my bedside to speak to me. I keenly recall the flight crew of Aero Med standing in their uniforms at my bedside. The flight crew encouraged me to get well and promised once I was stable and off oxygen, they would take me up again in the helicopter. I was told that I was one of the first children the trauma team had encountered because the Aero Med program was fairly recent. They regularly checked in on me to monitor my progress.

At my mother's command, since I was a minor, several people were turned away and not allowed to visit. This is my recollection and testimony from many individuals regarding her behavior. However, she did allow a few people to come without hesitation, including my grandpa Ron and his wife, Ann, and one of Ivan's brothers and his wife and children. I am thankful for each and every visit. It brought me great joy knowing they cared. Once I was out of intensive care, and per the physician's suggestion, I had more contact with the outside world. A few of my closest friends came to visit as often as their parents would drive them to the hospital. I was so full of joy seeing them and just being a teenage girl with them.

On one occasion, I received a card from fellow classmates. There were many signatures and encouraging words. However, one individual wrote, "That's what you get for driving." It was distressing. This person didn't know my story. From that moment, I decided I was never returning to Zeeland Public Schools.

Independence Day

Around that time, I remember randomly seeing my stepfather's face near the end of my bed. I cannot say for certain if it was a fear-based or drug-induced vision, but I began having nightmares of him coming to the hospital to kill me. I am unsure of when I was told that he died. Shortly after the nightmares started, my mother gave me a Polaroid picture of my dead stepfather laying in a casket at the funeral home. As morbid as it may sound, it allowed me to *see* he *was* dead and realize he would not hurt me any longer. But as a result, I was left with tremendous emotional scars. I felt deep sadness and cried often when I looked at the picture. I still did not have any sort of closure. But there is one thing I did feel. On a day we celebrate freedom as a country, even though I was intubated and in critical care and fully dependent on others, *for the first time in my life, I felt safe, free from my abuser.*

At dusk, my nurses surprised me by strategically placing my bed near the window so I was able to observe the fireworks display in downtown Grand Rapids. This evening was full of emotions, but I felt safe and loved.

Abandoned and Depressed

My mother was not supportive in any fashion, and truly, I do not remember her being at the hospital more than a handful of times. When she did come, she would be found sitting in the smoking room with a cigarette in hand. My mother wanted no part of talking to me about the accident or about my stepfather. She would pop her head in now and then to make an appearance. She told me she was hiring a lawyer, mentioning that the accident was being investigated and that I may get into trouble. She said I was not to talk about it. I was full of fear. I didn't know what kind of trouble I could get into.

Meanwhile my little sister was staying with her aunt and uncle. Our mother was having a medical issue of her own. She had to undergo a hysterectomy, leaving her unable to have children in the future. My mother blamed me for this often. She was really giving me the cold shoulder when I needed her *now* more than ever in my whole life. Doctors, nurses, and a few immediate family members noticed how she behaved around me, and I felt the tension too. She had clearly rejected me and simply did not want to be around me. After the amputation, my mother had said to me, "I would kill myself if I had one leg." Laying in the hospital critically injured and ill, my life was forever changed. Once a scared little girl, now I was a teen facing the same loss of self-worth and lacking self-acceptance, mentally and physically. I had been abandoned.

Six weeks in, as requested by two treating physicians, a comprehensive evaluation was done to address "depression, grief, trauma, and pain." In my chart, the doctor noted the depression, saying, "Apparently has been seen by social services and psychology, but this child is severely depressed, long-range planning here important." The physician was correct. I was severely depressed. I had held on to what had happened to me for way too long. My mother knew about the abuse and did not protect me. And now she was telling me that I may get in trouble. I was devastated.

The physician noted that I was "verbal, polite, and tearful on occasion." He wrote, "trapped with father 1 ½ hrs. in car as father died." "Missed funeral." He also wrote, "post-trauma stress and grief secondary to depression related to father and anxiety regarding body, walking, return to school and walking." His plan listed many therapies, including "deep relaxation techniques, use of the pain thermometer, massage on arms, neck, back, focus on nurturing the 'parts that work okay.'" He also recommended talking with female counselors and to have "social contact with friends, view letters, visits and calls."

My mother did not want to acknowledge *anything* that had happened to me. She refused to let me talk to her about anything. But I was not going to keep it to myself any longer. I confided to the female counselors about the abuse that had happened to me before the accident. When my mother became aware of this information, she visited less often and called instead. Because of what I disclosed, I was sent to get a CT of my abdomen and pelvis. Aside from finding resolving hematomas, they discovered clear evidence of the abuse I had endured.

Angels of Light

For weeks I tried to grasp the severity of my situation, as nobody was certain when speaking to me. It was literally one minute at a time, one hour at a time, one day at a time. I now believe the lack of communication was intentional so I would remain hopeful and look forward to each day. The hospital's chaplains stopped in my room frequently and prayed with me. I looked forward to visiting with them because they encouraged me in the moment and promised to come back. And they did. We talked about God. I knew God was with me and He had saved me, but what I did not understand is why my mother didn't love me or have any compassion for me, *ever*. Nobody could answer that. I cried before God often, wondering about this, but I never did get an answer.

Ann, Grandpa Ron's wife, would come and decorate my windows with seasonal cling-on decorations and just sit with me. Their investment of self and time is forever treasured in my heart. One nurse who took care of me in the critical care unit bought me a Precious Moments plaque reading, "All Things Are Possible, Only Believe." I knew this was true, and I was determined to persevere, knowing God was with me. I still have this plaque hanging on my wall today. God was using His angels on earth to remind me He was there.

Helpless and Exposed

My body was only lightly covered over certain areas because of the remaining required traction and continual cleaning and changing of bandages. I had no privacy. My body was exposed to whoever was assigned to me, day or night, man or woman. Being a trauma victim, I experienced anger when the male doctors, interns, or nurses had access to freely lift my covers, exposing my female body parts. I had no control, as I was at their mercy. I fully understood they were there to help me, but it felt so violating, absolutely daunting.

Once the catheter was removed and I was able to use a bedpan, I became angrier. Now, I had to push the call button and wait. *Wait to be violated*. That's how I felt. While I was truly grateful for the help, I felt many emotions as the assistant helped me on and off the bedpan, wiping and cleaning. Even the care provided when I was menstruating fully degraded me. It enraged me. I did not share that frustration with anyone because *I did not trust anyone.* I was in a vulnerable position due to the situation I was in, but the staff had no idea. Being help-less and exposed after being abused was another moment in life that I could not change.

Biological Bonding

When the accident occurred, my biological father, Bob, was noti-fied and gained entry into my life as a result. Prior to the accident, I did not have a relationship with him, but now he was insistent on being in my life. My mother detested the fact that he had reentered my life, more so that he was at the hospital often. It was tense at times.

Despite the tension, I began to develop a relationship with Bob. I was cautious but believed that because he was my "real" father, he would not hurt me. Once I was transferred from the surgical criti-cal care unit and placed in the pediatric unit where family members were permitted to stay overnight, he stayed overnight a lot, frequently missing work. Part of me was happy, but inside I felt torn, knowing he had a wife, children, and stepchildren at home he was neglecting. Also, knowing my mother was irate about him being there made my teenage life all the more dysfunctional.

My father and I bonded over music. One day he brought a VHS tape for us to watch. It was an Iron Maiden concert. He would often bring up his music on cassettes and have me listen to it with him. *Crazy, loud, screaming* heavy metal bands that I was unaware of until he intro-duced them to me. He repeatedly played his music, and eventually, it began to grow on me. Some of his favorite bands became mine too. It was not the kind of music I would have ever listened to, but because I wanted to identify with him, I became interested in whatever he brought. Soon I was learning to play chess and bumper pool. Hour after hour, and all hours of the night, we played both. Afterward we would go to the cafeteria and eat during the third shift and end up in the canteen where he would smoke his cigarettes.

While I was excited for a chance to get to know my biologi-cal father, and I did enjoy our time together, I was sometimes uncomfortable in his presence. Specifically, when he made inappropriate comments and flirted with my nurses. One particular night, I turned my head and looked through the side rail of my hospital bed, and there he laid on a rollaway cot in his underwear. I was horrified. I was embarrassed, too, as nurses came in and out, tending to my beeping machines while he slept through it. I remember apologizing to one nurse because she was disgusted when she noticed him. The look on her face made me aware that I did not yet know this man, and even at age fourteen, I was unsure of this behavior.

Helicopter Promise

For months, the Aero Med trauma team monitored my progress. The time had arrived. I was finally stable. The flight crew obtained permission from my mother and physicians to take another flight on the helicopter; this one I voluntarily accepted. I was excited.

I was transported on a stretcher by ambulance from Butterworth Hospital to the Kent County International Airport where the helicopter and crew were waiting. My father was allowed to go on this flight with me. He was seated in the physician's seat, and I was secured in place on the stretcher, positioned slightly different as I was the day of my life-saving transport. We were given headsets to wear so we could hear each other talking. Once the helicopter started up, my recollection of the past events was stimulated, bringing me right back to my traumatic experience. The noise of the engine, the blades swirling, the vibration, and the lifting off the ground flooded my mind with painful memories. It almost overwhelmed me, but I quickly refocused. This time, I knew I was safe. The pilot circled the airport, allowing us to see for miles and take in the surrounding beauty. Afterward, I was transported back to Butterworth Hospital. I am truly grateful for the unforgettable opportunity, a promise fulfilled.

No Other Option but to Move On

After four months had passed since the accident, it was late fall, and my doctors really could not do anything more for me. Although my legs were still oozing with infection, they decided to have me evaluated by a physician from Mary Free Bed Rehabilitation Hospital. On the day the physician arrived to do this special examination, my team of doctors was present. This male doctor looked just like my stepfather. I started to panic.

As you can imagine, fear and anger resurfaced. My injuries were so massive and high up my thighs that there was no way to cover my female body parts. Knowing that he was going to see me fully naked and inflict pain upon me while my wounds were unpacked and repacked, I felt instant hatred! I *did not* want him examining me.

Against my will, the team administered the IV medications, including Versed, and began the excruciating process. I had no choice or voice. I don't have total recall after that. However, the consultation states that upon examination and despite direction, I showed inappropriate behavior, exposing myself. Due to the sexual abuse, the doctor expected that I would need long-term counseling, but my mother did not get me any outside help for those issues.

Following the doctor's exam, he assessed I would be much better served at Mary Free Bed Rehabilitation Hospital. Later in October, I was discharged from Butterworth Hospital and transferred by ambulance.

Although my medical situation improved significantly from admission, my left femur developed osteomyelitis. My orthopedic surgeon remained active in my care because, back then, there was no cure for osteomyelitis, only treatment. My body was slowly healing, and I was happy to be moving on to the next part of my journey. I have such deep gratitude for every staff member who assisted in saving my life, caring for my physical body, and continuing to do his or her profession in the midst of my family dysfunction and chaos.

CHAPTER 4

A Spark of Hope

And now these three remain: faith, hope and love. But the greatest of these is love.
1 Corinthians 13:13

LIFE AT MARY FREE BED WAS DEPRESSING TO SAY THE LEAST. I FELT isolated and alone. I was placed in the pediatric unit in a private room and had a whole new set of faces to get used to, both men and women who were assigned to my specialized care. No overnight family visits were allowed.

The pediatric team and amputee team worked together to develop an effective treatment plan, which also included my mother. Initially, she participated but quickly detached and became uninvolved. Successful rehabilitation required family involvement. But I was a teen girl alone on this journey, an unaccompanied minor.

I still struggled with the rejection that I felt by my mother and the fact that every morning I would have to undress and transfer to a roll-in shower chair to wet the gauze and unpack the wounds myself so my treating physician could see them. I had to present myself half naked. I absolutely hated every moment of this process. Each time the doctor came in my bathroom, he would be singing the same song with a big grin on his face and look me over. I so desperately wanted a female doctor, but I had no choice. I settled in for the rehabilitation stay with little enthusiasm. For me, this was another thing to survive. I knew I'd get through it.

Morning after morning the embarrassment and anger resurfaced. The doctor would arrive, and the routine began. He started tapping on my residual limb to desensitize it. The pain was unbearable as elec-trifying sensations shot through my entire body.

One thing about amputation that many people don't realize is that the sensation of the limb "being there" is ever so present. The brain and spinal cord can mix signals alerting you that something isn't quite right, resulting in pain. Sometimes my leg itches uncontrollably. Most days I still feel my toes. Because I had bone just under the surface of my scarring, even the slightest touch would trigger "phantom" pain. I proclaim the pain is real. Three decades later, I sporadically experience bouts of phantom pain, lasting from minutes to hours.

As I met other patients and heard their stories of how they were injured, it was in the forefront of my mind not to share my details. My mother had repeatedly warned me not to talk about the acci-dent because I might get into trouble. I did not understand. I was so conflicted. I told the truth to law enforcement, everything I knew. But when other patients asked me about my accident and what happened, I lied out of shame. I said my stepfather grabbed the steering wheel. I did not want to have to explain each mortifying event that led to my hospitalization. I even justified the lie in my own mind as the drilling tape played over and over in my head of my stepfather saying, *"If you ever tell anybody, I will kill you." "I am not going to jail; I will kill us both first."*

For many abused children, lying is a means of survival, a way of self-protecting. For me, I was also afraid to get in trouble and disap-point my mother. Like I said, my life was dysfunctional, with a capital *D*. For a few years after the accident, when asked, I continued to lie. Today, I have revealed the truth of my story. No more shame. No more guilt. "Christ has set us free to live a free life. So take your stand! Never again let anyone put a harness of slavery on you" (Galatians 5:1 MSG).

Saving My Other Leg

Part of the process of someday returning home was to have our house modified. My mother was angry and made it known to me and those involved that she did not like people interfering with her life and changing her home. She did not want the accessible ramps on either side of her house nor the widening of the bathroom door. It was humiliating for her to have her house noticeably "handicapped."

Once our home was accessible, and when my mother actually agreed for me to come home for a weekend visit, home nursing care was also scheduled. My mother did not want any part in changing my dressings, as they had to be changed several times throughout the day and medication administered at precise times as well. However, she did not want the nurses at her home either. I felt rejected, like I was a heavy burden.

While I was excited to actually be home for my fifteenth birthday, I was not well. I lay in my bed with the chills and began to shake uncontrollably. My sister and mother brought me all the extra blankets in our house, but I was still so cold. I had a fever and could not stop shaking. I asked my mother to take me to the emergency room at Butterworth Hospital. She really did not want to. After all, soon she would be dropping me off at the rehabilitation hospital. Over and over I cried, begging her to take me. She called her friend and asked if she would ride along to the hospital. Thankfully, Vicki said she would. We drove to Grand Rapids. I was readmitted to Butterworth Hospital with infection flaring up in my body. The doctors did not know how to continue treatment for my left leg. Arrangements were made to get an evaluation at the Mayo Clinic in Rochester, Minnesota. I was scared. I *never* thought I would get better and be out of the hospital.

I remember this trip to the Mayo Clinic very well. My mother, her new husband, whom she married in Las Vegas while I was still unstable and inpatient, and I went to the Muskegon airport. It was winter, and it was my very first time in an airplane, a charter plane. Getting through security was an interesting and slow process. My wheelchair, internal clips, and leg brace added to the difficulty. My left leg was in a brace, sticking straight out, not able to bend at all. I had to transfer onto a tiny chair that could fit up the steps, while trusting complete strangers to carry and manipulate my body without banging my foot on anything. Once inside, I had to transfer again onto the seat and sit sideways with my leg stretching over onto the next seat. I was terrified. I sat near the back by myself. We flew to Chicago, Illinois, then transferred to another plane to get to Minnesota. The entire process was a great ordeal.

After we arrived at the airport, a taxi drove us to our hotel. Once we checked into our room, my mother and her husband decided to leave and go to a local bar. I was left unsupervised, in a new location, in another state. I laid down and listened to a Michael Jackson tape on my Walkman cassette player and eventually fell asleep. Words cannot express how alone I felt.

If you've never been to the Mayo Clinic, it's an intimidating and eye-opening experience. People come from all over the world looking for hope and answers to their healthcare situations. Mayo Clinic is known for their medical expertise and collaboration with teams of doctors. When you get evaluated, you receive so much more than a second opinion; you learn the best recommendations and options available for your specialized-care needs. The following morning and the next few days, I had numerous tests performed: X-rays, scans, lab draws, and so on. It was one appointment after another.

Days later, once all the test results were received and reviewed, we were called to return to Mayo Clinic. The specialists talked a lot about different scenarios due to the numerous injuries sustained to the entire left leg, my only remaining leg. The diagnosis was chronic osteomyelitis, which is a fancy word for a bone infection. Infections like this can happen when bone is exposed to bacteria and foreign objects due to injuries like I had sustained or when bacteria enters the bloodstream and spreads to tissue and bone. At that time, osteomyelitis was considered an incurable medical condition and was only treatable with heavy-duty intensive antibiotics, which I had endured for months with no success. The immediate solution presented to prevent the infection from spreading further was amputation.

The doctors left the room, allowing a time of discussion for us. I already felt despised and rejected by my mother because she said she would kill herself if she had only *one* leg. I could not imagine what she may say to me if I had the other leg amputated too. I cried out to my mother, "I would rather die first than to have no legs at all."

My mother knew the severity of the situation. With the possible outcomes of eventually losing my left leg due to death of the bone or infection spreading through my bloodstream and potentially causing death, my mother let me decide. I am grateful that she didn't care either way!

I was flown back to Michigan and readmitted to Butterworth Hospital to "wait and see" while attempting more treatments. The next several months were pain-filled as they performed intense debridements, cutting and removing dead muscle and tissue out of my left thigh wound in the hope of saving my leg. Several times daily I would have to undergo dressing changes for the wounds to be unpacked and cleaned and rewrapped.

One of the recommendations was a specialized monoplace hyperbaric chamber for daily therapy. For many weeks, I was put inside the chamber for treatment. Once fully enclosed and sealed in the chamber, it was filled with air pressure, three times higher than what we normally breathe in. I was offered gum to chew because the air pressure change was very hard on my ear drums; they popped and clogged while beginning and ending the treatment. The chewing distracted me and lessened the pressure in my ears and head. This process from beginning to end took approximately two and a half hours. As an individual with claustrophobia, I dreaded this treatment. This was a difficult time for me, but it was a necessity to gather and absorb more oxygen into my body to speed the healing process and fight the infection. I had such relief that the doctors at the Mayo Clinic were willing to try new additional therapies, and I was determined to push forward and get through whatever I had to for a chance at saving my leg. I had survived and endured up till this point; I was on a mission, and I was not looking back, no matter how hard or painful or difficult.

A New Calling

One of the hospital's chaplains, Adina, visited me often. She was a blessing to me. Each time she visited she would offer words of encouragement, bring me spiritual material to read, and just love on me. Before leaving, she would always pray with me. "Be joyful in hope, patient in affliction, faithful in prayer," she'd pray from Romans 12:12. I felt such comfort from her presence. During one visit in particular, she noticed I was depressed. There were many reasons for that. The lengthy hospitalization and no discharge estimation due to the infected wounds played a huge part in how I felt.

Another day she walked in my hospital room with a big smile on her face and asked, "Tracy, would you like to receive a phone call from a very special person long distance? Would you like to receive a phone call from Joni Eareckson Tada and talk to her?" I was overjoyed, because not long before this, Adina gave me the book *Joni: An Unforgettable Story*.

I was excited and felt special, realizing that I was going to speak with an actual author. What encouraged me most in talking with Joni is that she understood the lengthy hospitalization, the isolation, and the emotions a teenage girl endures following an accident causing disability. Although our disabilities are very different, we were able to identify with one another.

Joni and I joked about being "shorter" than other people and always having a crick in our neck as we looked up to have conversations. We also shared similar experiences in navigating our wheelchairs while learning to discern our surroundings.

Joni and I both knew that we could accept ourselves but weren't quite sure others could. I asked Joni if she was married. She was. I wasn't sure if *anyone* would like me, let alone one day marry me. I did not share that with Joni, but she continued saying how she gained security and meaning from God and not from other people. I held on to those words and felt hopeful. Even today the words Joni spoke into my life remain, although I did struggle for years trying to find my security in other things and people aside from God, but I was encouraged. From that moment on, I knew God was placing that calling in my heart to write a book as well—to become an author who hopefully inspires others.

Roaming My Hospital Home

Finally, the day came when I was able to leave my room. Once I was unhooked from the IV pump, and after my team of physicians made their daily rounds, I was given permission to roam around. I used a big, clunky standard wheelchair and left my room as often as possible. Day and night, I wheeled myself around the entire hospital, visiting every floor and area of the hospital that I was able, including revisiting the ICU unit. I was known by and knew many staff by name.

I enjoyed talking with people who were waiting for their loved ones to complete testing or recover from surgery. I watched patients come and go, whether they were healthy enough to be discharged or died as a result of an illness or injury. I found plenty of things to occupy my time. However, I had to be back in my room at certain times for medication, dressing changes, treatments, even schoolwork.

Arrangements were made to have a tutor come regularly to assist with my studies. Although I had sufficient time to learn and do homework, I had no desire whatsoever. I developed a spirit of rebellion, taking full advantage of my freedom to leave my room, and on a few occasions "skipped school." I knew when the tutor would be arriving and when I should be in my room. Instead, I would wheel myself through the hallways to the elevator and go sit outside near the entrance to the emergency room where security guards were assigned. I felt comfort and peace being near others in their time of medical need.

Eventually, I realized that avoiding the tutor was not going to benefit me. Even though the pain, medications, dressing changes, and treatments interfered throughout my day, my rebellion turned to determination to do what was necessary to graduate on time with my class.

As time progressed, and because of the chronic situation, I was given permission from staff to have my sister, Amy, who was only nine years old, stay with me. I was also encouraged to have friends stay, too, but only one person at a time. I was delighted.

My friends stayed overnight on occasion, but my sister stayed overnight frequently. Our mother would drive Amy up to the hospital, a thirty-minute drive, drop her off (sometimes with a plate of no-bake cookies), and return when the weekend was over. I absolutely enjoyed having my sister stay with me. She slept next to my hospital bed on a reclining chair. My mother must have had an arrangement with the hospital because my sister and my friends were given breakfast, lunch, a midday snack, and dinner while they stayed.

The environment was a hospital setting, but when I had my sister or a friend overnight, we each had our own wheelchair to ride around the hospital. We went to the canteens, gift shop, and cafeteria. Many times during the late-night hours, we raced the chairs through the hallways of the main floor and filled them with joyful laughter. We jammed out to the radio and sang aloud, had girl talk, styled our hair, and put on makeup. I could only wear shirts at this time because of my leg wounds and bandages, but I was at least able to look dressed from the waist up. I regained some normalcy, considering my reality.

I had an amazing nursing staff while I was an inpatient. Actually, I am forever grateful to each and every nurse who cared for me from day one, but I am going to be honest and say I did have a few that I highly favored. One nurse was my absolute favorite. She was the big sister I never had. Her name is Anita Grant. She showered me with love and compassion and made life enjoyable through the surprises and pranks that she and another nurse pulled on me quite often. Through the good days and not-so-good days, because of them, many were filled with joy and laughter. They amused me.

I met many people while lying in my hospital bed. Every day I would receive a midday snack (cheese and crackers) delivered by a guy who was a few years older than me. He noticed the '80s hair band pictures pasted all over my hospital room walls. Day after day we had conversations, with music being the main topic. We became friends. Jim brought me some cassette tapes with different songs he recorded of the bands he listened to, which soon became some of my favorites as well. Jim told me he could hear me listening to them whenever he walked by my room. Music was a big factor in our friendship, and thanks to social media, we have reconnected.

I was placed in several different private rooms on this floor. Ultimately, I ended up in a room at the end of the hall. This room had many windows. It was an especially large room compared to the other private rooms I had occupied. During all hours of the day, I listened to music. I played a variety of cassettes on my boombox and listened to them—*loudly!* When I wasn't playing my cassettes, I was listening to WKLQ, a local radio station. One day a few songs played in a row that I recognized from the roller rink. I began to cry, realizing that I would never be able to skate again. Then I heard the disc jockey announce the band was going to tour with the return of their "one-armed drummer"! What?! *How can he play drums with only one arm?* I thought to myself. From my hospital bed, I immediately opened my bedside drawer and grabbed the phone book. I called the radio station and asked to speak to the manager. I explained that I was also an amputee, an inpatient at the hospital, and had been for some time. I asked if he could get ahold of the drummer and ask him a question for me. I gave my contact information, including the hospital room number.

Many weeks passed, and then I received a surprise visit from Danny Douglas, the DJ from the radio station. He brought me a bunch of cassette tapes with the radio logo stickers in place and mentioned that he was able to contact the band's management. Danny asked me if I would like to meet Rick Allen, the one-armed drummer from Def Leppard. I was ecstatic! I loved this band's music, and they were very popular. I was thrilled, so of course I said, "Yes!" Danny told me he would keep in touch.

Gaining Independence

By June, the left thigh wound was still not healed, a whole year since the accident. My team of physicians at Butterworth felt there was no reason to keep me from learning how to be fully functioning as an amputee and self-sufficient at using a wheelchair. I returned to Mary Free Bed Rehabilitation Hospital. Once more the pediatric team and amputee team worked together on a treatment plan, but not surprisingly, my mother was not interested.

I settled into my environment and did what was asked, advocating for myself without any parental input. My daily schedule began after breakfast. In between dressing changes, my day was filled with schoolwork, physical therapy, occupational therapy, recreational therapy, social workers, prosthetic fittings, and driver's training. I had to learn how to drive a vehicle adapted with hand controls. I was fifteen years old and couldn't wait to get behind the wheel and drive again. I dreamed of the day when I would be independently driving, with the ability to listen to music and enjoy the surrounding beauty with no destination, just driving. I looked forward to this goal of freedom.

Today, driving is still one of my favorite things to do; it brings me joy, but truly only if I am driving. I do not enjoy others driving. It does not have anything to do with the individual's skills or ability. Even though I have been a passenger many times, I still feel uneasy, and more often than not, I cannot keep my mouth shut, like a back-seat driver. I cannot explain this sense of anxiety because I was the driver in my accident. When inside a vehicle, the need for control is still an ongoing issue that I am praying will resolve someday. I have been told its post-traumatic-stress related, which I can accept, but I refuse to take medication to assist in that. Never have. Never will. I am trusting God to sustain me through every ride as a passenger and that includes not saying a word to the driver, mainly my husband. There have been several occasions recently where I see God's healing hand in this situation. I am trusting and believing for His full deliverance.

I worked really hard at utilizing the prosthesis, but my left leg was still so weak. When I was in a standing position, the blood flow went through my left leg, causing it to change color and itch uncontrollably. I had to wear a brace on my left leg to keep the femur stable and prevent it from refracturing. The brace went from my foot, all the way up to wrap around my waist. It did have a locking device on the knee so I could unlock it to ambulate. The prosthesis hurt my residual limb. It was difficult and extremely uncomfortable, but I was determined. Through the tears and pain, I did the best I could with the limitations I had. I knew God saw everything and one day it would all be okay.

During both pediatric stays, I had several roommates. Although the majority of them had suffered a traumatic brain injury, two others did not. One girl, who I will call Daisy, was a paraplegic, and the other girl, who I will call Jasmine, had no arms. I became friends quickly with each girl due to the inpatient experience we shared. Daisy and I had a few things in common—we both used a wheelchair for mobility, and we turned to food to numb feelings. But I realized that was all we had in common. Daisy was an inpatient for the second time to encourage proper self-care as she was unable to feel her bladder or bowels. She was not motivated in any way to help herself except when it came time to eat. Her upper body and arms were fully functioning, but her spirit was unwilling. She complained her way through every day and played a victim of her circumstance. Due to the lack of commitment in hygiene, we were not roommates long.

Jasmine and I both had missing limbs and shared a common spirit of determination. As we ate our breakfast together, I watched her pick up the utensils with both feet and dig in. Then she brushed her hair and teeth. I was in awe at the things she could do, and I never heard her complain.

I learned a great deal of how others lived with the disabilities they were born with or incurred as a result of illness or injury. Although I felt "normal" and accepted by my roommates, I wondered what life would be like outside those walls.

Hysteria and Hope

Toward the end of the summer, with permission from my physician, I was allowed to leave the rehabilitation hospital with a nurse for a special prearranged meeting in Ionia, Michigan. I requested my favorite nurse, Anita, to accompany me. I was invited to meet and speak with Rick Allen, Def Leppard's drummer. I was excited, also a bit nervous, as I watched Rick walk toward me. I was even more surprised when I noticed he had freckles because I didn't see any in the magazine pictures or posters. We introduced ourselves and vulnerably shared our stories.

Rick was beyond determined to play the drums even after losing his arm, and with his customized drum kit, he was able to persevere. He shared that this was his first tour, Hysteria World Tour, since losing his left arm due to the injuries he sustained in a car accident. And then I asked him the question that I so longed to ask, "How do you dare go in front of people with only one arm?" At that moment, I really didn't care about anything else.

You see, my mother had fully rejected me saying, *"I would kill myself if I had one leg."* That one comment she made over a year ago haunted me every day, attempting to define who I was and how I should feel about myself. I had no idea what my life would be like outside of the hospital setting. I felt accepted at both the hospital and the rehabilitation hospital, but how was I going to feel accepted by others if my own mother didn't accept me? I mentioned that I was afraid to go back to school, unsure of how people were going to react to me. Teary-eyed, Rick said, "You just do it. We are no different." And then I noticed the back of his T-shirt, "TAKE NO SHIT." These three words remained with me. I often repeated that phrase to myself for encouragement to persevere. I was determined to be stronger and more courageous than my mother. She was in an abusive second marriage, enduring verbal and physical abuse from her alcoholic husband. I was taking my life back and *nobody* was going to take advantage of me in *any possible way, again, ever!*

I had never been to a concert before, and now here I was, backstage, meeting all the members of Def Leppard. I was astounded. We took more pictures, and he gave me some signed memorabilia, a vinyl twelve-inch *Hysteria* picture disc, and a couple of copies of *The Def Leppard Story: Animal Instinct* by David Fricke.

Before the show, I was carried up a flight of stairs by security to a covered area which stood near the stage. I was accompanied by my nurse and Rick, briefly. While the crowd looked, they cheered. I felt special and accepted. The band Europe opened for Def Leppard. I had the perfect view. The concert was loud. It was fantastic!

Through Rick's kindness and encouragement, and Def Leppard's music, I was inspired *that day* to move forward and step out. He taught me to appreciate what I have even more. He encouraged me not to take life for granted; to modify and try new things in order to be efficient; never to forget what I have been through; and to keep moving forward. This was a big deal for me—it impacted my teenage years tremendously. Words cannot express the gratitude I have for the life-changing inspiration that I absorbed. Later that evening, I returned to Mary Free Bed Rehabilitation Hospital. Little did I know that I was nearing the time when I would go home to figure out life as an amputee on my own. I had absolutely no idea that I would have to cling to Rick's words of encouragement, as the things he taught me would be harder than I could have imagined. But I held his words close to my heart during what would become some of the hardest days yet to endure—trying to find my way in the world as a young disabled girl.

I had been hospitalized for 437 consecutive days, and for the first time in a while, I had *hope*.

I will thank You forever, because You have done it, [You have rescued me and kept me safe]. I will wait on Your name, for it is good, in the presence of Your godly ones.

Psalm 52:9 (AMP)

CHAPTER 5

Unwelcomed Home

But you, LORD, are a shield around me,
my glory, the One who lifts my head high.

Psalm 3:3

I RETURNED HOME . . .

Except this was not *my* home.

From the moment I rolled across the threshold of the front door, it was clear I was not welcome. My mother had married an alcoholic, and she became one too. For over a year, this man had lived in our home with my mother and sister. Life went on without me. Although the surroundings were familiar, it felt as if I was a complete stranger. Who was I kidding? I *was*, even to myself.

There was nothing anyone could do to heal my wounds any quicker. Upon discharge, a detailed plan was established so I could continue to receive outpatient services at the local hospital.

Initially, my mother paid a female acquaintance to come sit with me while she was at work, but it didn't last long and she stopped coming. This individual was the one I chose to disclose the abuse to my mother in front of years earlier, trusting she would help me. I was wrong. I was not pleased to see her.

Five days a week, I attended occupational therapy and physical therapy. I went alone. I was not interested in the prosthetic leg, and the bulky left leg brace was uncomfortable. Walking hurt my left knee, and the hard material of the prosthetic stabbed into my groin. It was awful. Because of the pressure placed against the scar tissue, each time I removed the prosthesis, my skin underneath had to be treated.

In-home nursing care was scheduled several times daily to unwrap, unpack, clean, and change the wound dressings. It was a very slow and painful process of healing from the bone outward.

Each time a nurse arrived when my mother was home, she tried to appear involved. But when nobody was around, I was ignored. My mother said she should do my wound dressings so that people would get out of her life and give her privacy.

After one of my visits, the nurse noticed my left leg had swelled and my residual limb had blisters. She scheduled an appointment for me to see the doctor. Because my mother did not attend, a phone call was made to her. When my mother was asked about the condition of my wounds, she reported that the blisters had disappeared.

My mother lied. She just wanted the professionals out of her home. I knew that, so I learned how to do my own wound cleaning and rewrapping. I was not going to allow my mother to stick her nicotine-covered fingers inside my wounds anyway.

Could It Get Any Worse?

My days were filled with appointments. While Amy was in school, an ambucab would pick me up and drive me to and from each appointment. Depending on the visit and which physician I was going to, an assigned nurse case manager would attend also because my mother was not involved.

My nights were filled with abuse, a different kind of abuse this time, but abuse all the same. My second stepfather was physically abusive to my mother and verbally abusive to us all. When he was sober, between the time he arrived home from work and 6:00 p.m., he was seemingly nice and soft-spoken, but that was always short-lived. On the evenings my parents stayed home, and after the drinking began, my stepfather would change into a completely different person. He was loud and assertive, argumentative, enraged. His face transformed so quickly, from an evil grin to a sudden outburst of laughter and back to a serious scowl. Even the look in his eyes was different. He was a bully, calling me a one-legged slut. My mother did not stop him. At times she chimed in, blaming me for killing Ivan and for what he did to me all those years as a child. She also blamed me for her inability to have more children. A lot of hurtful things spewed out of her mouth. I would retreat to my bedroom and remain with the door closed until morning. Amy joined me most of the time. I would often have her sneak out and get snacks. She was quick and able to go unnoticed.

My mother and stepfather gambled often. Many weeknights after work, they went to Bingo. On the weekends, they went to a casino. A few times they even flew to Las Vegas, leaving me home to babysit Amy. I was often alone babysitting her, but I was also allowed to have a friend overnight. When us kids were left alone, we jammed out to music, called the radio station and requested songs, ate whatever we were allowed to eat, and sang on my mother's karaoke machine. Those were good times, some of the best memories I have as a teen, filled with joy and laughter.

Determined to Learn

A plan to return to school was mentioned, and we scheduled a tour at the Zeeland High School. On that day, my mother, nurse case manager, and I were greeted by the individual who was giving the walk through. As we went from one area of the school to another, I noticed a few classmates who I had not seen or talked to since before the accident. All I could think of was what their thoughts were toward me and who it was that wrote the cruel message on the card I received while in critical care. Written or spoken, words have the ability to change the outcome of a situation. They can lift us up and encourage us, or they can knock us down and discourage us. The Bible tells us in Proverbs, "The tongue has the power of life and death, and those who love it will eat its fruit" (18:21). Words are powerful. I was haunted by that message from an unknown classmate, and I was still adamant about not returning.

A few of my friends were also there to say hi, and although I was happy to see them, I knew I was not enrolling at this school. After the tour, my mother and I went home. When I was told the starting date,

I informed her I was not planning to go. I only went along with this to please everyone else. I was stubborn and planned to learn at home. My mother and nurse case manager made a bargain with me. They offered to have transportation pick me up and bring me back home if I would agree to attend another public high school in the next town over. I agreed. This was a huge school with crowded hallways. I often had to wait for the halls to be cleared of students to allow room for me to get from one class to another, leaving me last to enter the classroom and make a scene as the teacher had students move so I could maneuver my wheelchair to a desk near the door. I was self-conscious and lacked confidence. I told my mother and case manager, and their solution was to have me sit in one classroom for most of the day to do my studies. Although there were other students in this classroom, this was not the solution nor the environment I needed. I was not intellectually handicapped.

I did make an attempt at attending this public high school, but it was not ideal. Four days in a row, the driver of a short yellow school bus beeped outside of my home. I refused to go. In fact, I threatened to drop out of school on my sixteenth birthday. When my dad heard this, he was mad and stopped talking to me. That was hurtful because he didn't listen to understand me; he only heard that I was quitting school.

The only time I noticed my mother's involvement was during this school situation. She did not want to get in any kind of trouble for me not attending school. Soon after that, a tutor began coming to our home several times a week to help catch me up on my studies. I was dedicated. I was excited to share the news with my dad. I called him, and we began talking on the phone regularly once again. He invited me to come and watch his band practices. On occasion my mother allowed me to go with him. I enjoyed those times very much.

Freedom Restored

Many weeks earlier I was evaluated at Mary Free Bed through a specialized driving rehabilitation program. I had learned how to drive a car with hand controls. There were many mechanical recommendations on which types of cars I could drive and several steps to learning how to get in and out of the car independently with my manual wheelchair. It was quite an ordeal.

First of all, the car had to be a two-door vehicle with an automatic transmission, power steering, power brakes, and a bench seat. To begin, I would roll up to the car and open the car door, and while holding the car door with one hand, I would roll my wheelchair back with my other hand to allow room for me to move forward near the driver's seat. My wheelchair had to be strategically placed as close to the car body as possible without nicking it, which I did many times, even chipping paint off my wheelchair frame. Once I had locked the brakes on my wheelchair, I then reached over with my right hand to grasp and tilt the steering column upward to make room for me as I transferred onto the driver's seat. It was quite an effort since my right hand, wrist, arm, and shoulder were basically dragging the weight of my body from the wheelchair onto the seat while my left hand, wrist, arm, and shoulder stabilized me every few inches during the transfer. At times it was comical when either arm gave out due to fatigue; my backside would drop between the wheelchair and the side of the driver's seat, landing on the bottom of the car doorjamb. Not only did it startle me and hurt, but on a few occasions, I came very close to peeing my pants. After that happened it was even more of an effort to transfer, but I always managed.

Once fully inside the car, I leaned over to my wheelchair and pulled the cushion off and set it inside the car. Then I grabbed the center of my wheelchair seat and lifted it to collapse my chair so I could prepare it for loading. I scooted my backside across the bench to the passenger's seat, while my legs remained on the driver's seat. I then leaned over and folded the driver's seat forward toward the steering wheel, then had to stretch out to reach and grasp the wheelchair and pop the front wheels up to the entrance of the back seat. Grasping the frame of my chair, I pulled it into the back-seat area. Finally, it was in. Then I pushed the driver's seat back, scooted over to the driver's seat once again to close the driver's door, and put my seat belt on. Ta-da! It was all so exhausting, and I'm sure anyone watching me would realize I was an independent person with tremendous determination.

After checking the mirrors, I started up the car and put it in drive. The gear shifter was on the right side of the steering column, but the hand controls that operated the accelerator and brake were located on the left side of the steering column, attached just a tad lower than the steering wheel itself. I had a spinner knob placed on the steering wheel for safety; it's similar to what you may have noticed on a semi driver's steering wheel. To accelerate, I pulled the handle toward me, and to brake, I pushed the handle away from me. The device was referred to as push/pull hand controls. The entire process of learning to independently load and unload my wheelchair and learn how to drive safely with hand controls took some time and a fair amount of effort, but my upper body was strong from the exercises learned and done while at Mary Free Bed. I was overjoyed at the ability to do it all by myself.

I passed the road test utilizing hand controls, and on my sixteenth birthday, I obtained my driver's license. But I was not satisfied. I desperately wanted to look like a normal teenager when I drove a car. I didn't want to have to use my hands to operate a vehicle. I called my driving instructor and made an appointment. I requested that he reevaluate my ability to use a left-foot accelerator because my left knee was now able to bend to ninety degrees, sufficient enough to use my left leg for driving. I worked really hard at home doing my physical therapy exercises to get to this point. Today that is still as far as my knee bends because of the injuries sustained. I am not complaining. I am ever so grateful to have my leg.

I was given the opportunity to have another assessment. I did have additional training to get familiar with the left-foot accelerator and using the regular brake with my left foot, but it came very naturally. I did not have any problems in positioning or reaction time. I completed the training program once again and passed the road test with the license bureau. I was now going to be using a left-foot accelerator instead of hand controls.

Anyone who has ever worked with the DMV can probably guess that this amount of testing and training wasn't easy. I was proud of myself because I took initiative to attempt a major hurdle and accomplished it. I was one step closer to independence. Now all I needed was a car.

Petition Permitted

Although I was a licensed driver, I was not able to drive just any vehicle. I began searching through the free auto/RV books for used cars that fit the description allowed for the adaptive equipment recommendations. I asked my mother to help me get a car. She was more than willing to permanently get rid of the ambucab transportation service people, so she petitioned the court to withdraw money. I had always wondered where money for the things I needed came from—I mean, was there a special fund of some kind the courts used for kids like me? But later I learned that it was from the lawsuit my mother had mentioned when I was hospitalized.

Over the course of my life, I had heard many rumors from friends and family about the accident and my part in it. Often times, there was a grain of truth but so distorted too. Some of the stories were utterly ridiculous. I was able to laugh at many of them, but a few gave me anxiety and deep pain. One news article headline I discovered over two *decades* after the accident made me cry. It came from *Weekly World News*.

"Teen Sues Dead Dad after Crash"

Fifteen-year-old Tracy Jane Van Order—who was driving when her stepdad was killed in a car crash—is suing him because he let her drive when she was too young.

Tracy, now of Grand Haven, Mich., was just fourteen when her stepdad Ivan Van Order let her drive.

Driving downhill on a gravel road, Tracy lost control and the car rolled over and smashed into some trees.

Van Order died at the scene. Tracy had to have her right leg amputated above the knee and her left leg was severely damaged.

Now Tracy is suing her stepdad's estate for her injuries (August 9, 1988).[2]

I experienced so much grief after reading this, but then I knew the truth. Almost immediately after the car accident, my mother had retained an attorney. She told me this early on in my hospitalization; however, I did not understand the necessity. The services and medical bills for my injuries would be paid through her insurance company for life. I also learned that I received a settlement, but monies were not available until I reached eighteen years of age.

I was shocked that our accident made the *Weekly World News* and saddened by the misrepresentation. I was still an inpatient when this article was printed. I was angry, and I cried when I thought about the headline. Ivan *was not* my dad. He *was* my stepfather. He *did not* adopt me. I am uncertain of the date of my last name change, but I do recall my mother saying that it was changed so we would appear to be an "organic" family.

The judge granted our petition for funds, and it didn't take me much time to locate a vehicle within the budget range given. I was on top of the world. My first car was a 1983 Chevrolet Monte Carlo with T-tops and a cassette player. I had a portable CB radio in the car for emergency communication—no cell phones back then. But before I had access to the car, it was fitted with the proper equipment by Clock Conversions (currently Clock Mobility), a left-foot pedal accelerator.

My mother arranged a deal at the nearest full-service gas station. Whenever I needed gas, I would go there, my tank would be filled, and the amount added onto the account. The bill was sent to our home monthly.

Once the car was adapted to suit my needs, my mother and step-father drove me to get it. I was so excited! I followed them home all the way from Grand Rapids only to learn once I got there that I was not allowed to park in the driveway. I had to park across the street from our home in a parking lot. It was *winter* . . . in *Michigan*. It was a struggle to wheel through the parking lot to the sidewalk across the street and up our inclined driveway *without snow*, so you can imagine what it was like with all the snow. But I accepted it. At least I now had a vehicle, and with it came much freedom. I gained a whole new level of independence and more hope.

Numbing Out

Three months had passed since discharge. I was not using the prosthesis as directed by the physical therapist. I had no desire. As I was often in my bedroom, there simply was no room to practice and maneuver sufficiently. Also, I was avoiding the criticism and name-calling from my stepfather. And my left leg was not completely healed, although wound bandages were no longer needed. Nurses slowly stopped coming to monitor my wound care, and antibiotics were discontinued. I was overjoyed. My mother was too.

I did not need to wear the left leg brace at all times, only when I stood up or used my prosthetic leg to walk. I decided to stop going to outpatient therapy. I had no support or encouragement to continue. I felt so alone. When I was home by myself, in spite of the physical pain, I did the best I could at learning how to walk.

Before the accident, our home was unloving, unaccepting, and uninviting. The memories of what happened before the accident would come flooding back as if all of it had just taken place. My mother would not talk to me or allow me to seek counseling. My physician offered counseling services, but instead I chose to share what I was going through at the moment with my nurse case manager. She did the best she could to encourage me and gave me additional school options. I had great pain, physical wounds that were visible, and mental and emotional wounds that were not. I was broken.

I returned to school at an alternative high school. I transported myself to and from school, a thirty-minute drive each way. I attended, but it was a hard environment. Most of the students came from a dysfunctional family background like me, but I was the only physically disabled individual using a wheelchair. I felt accepted by everyone because we each had a story.

Many weekends friends came with me to my dad's band practices where underage drinking was allowed. My biological father had sexual interactions and relations with a couple of the girls. Although the girls expressed an interest and fondness about my dad, I despised it. I was happy that the girls were happy but sickened by the whole situation. I was once again placed in the middle of another dysfunctional situation; one I had no control over. It was not appropriate. He was a married man. The girls were insecure, vulnerable, and seventeen years of age and under. I lost all respect for him. I think I just kept going as a way to numb out the pain; it was one way of distracting me from the pain I was experiencing in every aspect of my life. Loud music helped with that—I loved it.

About this time, I began talking with my stepsiblings. My mother was not happy at all about us reconnecting. But weekend after weekend, and on the condition that I took Amy along, she did allow me to drive to Bloomingdale to visit. I also reconnected with the Michaud twins, Robert and Albert. The only stipulation was that I return by curfew on Sundays and I continue with school. My mother didn't care about my school attendance; she was more concerned with how she appeared to the many professionals in my life and didn't want to look like a "bad mom." Boy, was she ever self-centered. I had no parental guidance, but I knew I wanted better for myself.

When my father and my mother forsake me, then the LORD will take care of me.
Psalm 27:10 (NKJV)

CHAPTER 6

Playing House

In their hearts humans plan their course,
but the LORD establishes their steps.

Proverbs 16:9

SCHOOL WAS OUT FOR THE WEEK, AND IT WAS A FRIDAY. MY STEP-
sister—who was my age, sixteen—and I had planned to hang out that
weekend; she had a babysitter for her daughter, who was not yet a
year old, and Amy was with her friend. I drove over an hour to get to
the home of my stepsister's grandparents, where she and her brothers lived. We decided to go to my dad's band practice at a home in
Holland, about a forty-five-minute drive. Robert, the eldest of the
Michaud twins, was visiting, so I invited him to join us. He and my
youngest stepbrother came along. Later that evening, for the second
time, Robert and I began dating.

A lot happened throughout the next several weeks. The chaos
at home was the same. I attended a follow-up appointment with my
physician, you guessed it, alone. I was there to basically say I was not
coming any longer. My physician was not pleased when I entered the
room in my wheelchair. I told him that I had not been wearing the
prosthetic because of difficulties at home and the fact that I spent as
little time as possible there. He knew the situation at my home was
beyond dysfunctional due to the lack of support while I was an inpatient. I told him that my schooling was going well and I was getting
A's in all subjects, except one, so I had to return to summer school
once more to catch up. He was extremely impressed with my progress

overall, given the adversities I had to overcome, and said that I had matured greatly over the past year with respect to developing realistic ways of coping with my situation. Then he mentioned further options for foster care but wanted my mother present for that conversation. Because my mother did not attend the appointments, she received summary reports in the mail. I knew she was aware of what was said during my appointments, but it didn't matter to me because it was the truth; it was our reality. I was discharged from outpatient physical therapy and scheduled another follow-up appointment with the idea that my mother would attend.

During school weeks, Robert and I wrote letters back and forth and talked on the phone. But once school let out on Fridays, I drove straight to his home. Amy was spending more time with her friends. so I did not have to bring her along. Robert and I were infatuated with each other. We spent as much time together as possible, often hanging out with my stepsiblings down the road.

Even though we were not sexually active, I wanted to be safe when I did make that choice. I requested to be put on birth control. My mother wanted *nothing* to do with me or talking to the doctor, but she did take me to that appointment. She did not want me speaking to *anyone about anything*. I was a disruption in her life, which she made known frequently by threatening to send me away. One evening, she did just that when I missed my curfew by ten minutes. Considering the drive was almost an hour from Robert's home, I was surprised when my mother told me I had to move out. I was only sixteen for one thing, and never mind my physical challenges. It was a lot to take in.

The following day I drove back to Bloomingdale and told Robert. I had no idea of where to go except to ask if I could move in with him. Robert had me ask his dad, who everyone called Shorty. So, I did. Shorty and I seemed to have an instant connection when I first met him three years earlier, back when I was thirteen. I guess I sort looked to him as a father figure. Knowing the situation, he agreed to let me move in.

Initially, I was overtaken by the presence of Robert's parents. His father, whose name was actually Albert, was a retired veteran, and his mother, Phyllis, was a stay-at-home mom. I admired them. Robert and Albert were juniors in high school by then. Every morning their father was up early with a cup of coffee and cigarette in hand. Shorty had an internal clock that impressed me. He never used an alarm and would always wake his boys up for school. I felt safe, secure, and completely accepted by each member of Robert's family.

I enjoyed the family environment, too, but their house was not accessible for anyone disabled. It had stairs at both entrances, no ramps or rails. Many times I had assistance entering and exiting the home, but it was a demanding task. When I didn't have help, I learned to transfer onto the stairs, open the door, lift my wheelchair up and over my head, set it inside the doorway, and proceed to lift myself up and transfer back into the wheelchair. It was physically demanding to say the least. The bathroom door was not wide enough to enter either, but I made it work. Each time I needed to use the bathroom, I would park my wheelchair as close to the door entry as possible, lock my brakes, and stand up by holding on to the doorway. I would hop a little to move into the bathroom. While balancing, I would twist my upper body and bend over, grab my wheelchair cushion off, and collapse the wheelchair so it would fit through the doorway. Then I would push the chair back to a seated position, replace the cushion, and sit down, closing the bathroom door behind me. The process repeated itself when exiting the bathroom. *Every day* was a struggle, but I settled in to survive once again. I had no other option. Although I was relieved to move out of the home situation I was in, I was conflicted too. This was not the future I envisioned.

Because I was a disabled child, my mother received money from the Social Security Administration. With the monthly disability check, she continued to pay my car insurance and monthly gas bill and gave me the remaining funds. I then gave Robert's parents seventy-five dollars a month for letting me live there. I learned a lot about Robert's family while living under the same roof. They were the poorest people I knew. I soon realized there was over a two-decade age gap between Robert's unmarried parents. They were both unemployed. His father, born in Lawrence, Massachusetts, is a veteran of World War II and the Korean War. He served in both the United States Navy and the United States Army. He received military veteran's benefits, and Robert's mother received supplemental security income (SSI) due to cognitive limitations.

Monthly, when their checks arrived, they had a routine. They would cash their checks, go to the post office to have the post office employee make out money orders to pay their bills, head to the grocery store to purchase groceries for the *entire month,* and drive home to put them away. Then off to the bar they went. They paid their monthly bar tab off and drank beer all evening long and did it again day after day until the funds were gone. Smoking cigarettes and drinking beer was their priority.

Robert's father was an alcoholic, a married man with five children when he began an affair with Robert's mother. Phyllis was born in Plainwell, Michigan, to alcoholic parents who neglected all their children. She dropped out of school in the seventh grade and never obtained a driver's license. The two of them moved in together, and Phyllis got pregnant. For the first years of the boys' lives, they carried their mother's maiden name. Eventually, they went through a legal name change to have their father's last name, Michaud. Robert's father became a widower years later, with no intention of marrying Phyllis. This was indeed a generational sin pattern both sons were living under. The thing about generational sin is that it's never easy to break free from the examples you've been given by those who raise or influence you. It would be much easier to fall in line with what you've been taught and shown, following the natural course of your life path. To radically change the outcome and direction of your life takes grit and determination. Robert and I sure had our work cut out for us.

Although I was unsure of many things, I was determined to have a better life than this. I would catch up with my graduating class if it killed me. While I attended summer school, Robert worked. I had over an hour drive one way to school, which gave me a lot of time to think about my new life situation. I knew that God was not pleased with me. Here I was, living with my boyfriend in a place where underage drinking was allowed, and by then, we were having sexual intercourse. We did not have any rules. I knew that God loved me, but deep down, I knew that He did not approve. I carried this heaviness alone, because everywhere I looked, all I noticed was the "anything-goes" attitude and lifestyle.

Robert and I had many conversations about our families and backgrounds. We knew as teenagers that none of this was right. Robert and I had no desire to be anything like our parents. We often discussed our future, and graduating was of utmost importance to us both. We talked about being parents ourselves one day and what that would look like, seeing how neither of us had invested parents. We even discussed the possibility of our relationship not working out and how we would co-parent, both resolving to remain fully involved no matter what the situation. We promised each other we would always place our child or children first, determining to be the best parents we possibly could be. Robert and I wanted to provide a future filled with structure and security.

Even though I appreciated Robert's parents taking me in, I had a strong desire to live in a home of my own, and I shared this with my mother. She was more than willing to petition the court on my behalf because it didn't look good that I was living in a handicapped-inaccessible home. The petition was granted.

I bought a single-wide trailer in Shangrai La Mobile Home Community located in Saugatuck, Michigan. Robert and I moved in and continued to make plans for our future. He enrolled at Saugatuck High School for his senior year, tried out for the basketball team, and made the cut. He also got a job at Perry Drug's Pharmacy. Robert worked as many hours as possible in between school, practices, and games. He was a hard worker, and I admired him a lot for that. I had planned to continue at the alternative high school for my junior year.

As my priorities changed, the communication with my friends changed too. I lost contact with some of them but remained connected to a few.

My mother contacted the Social Security Administration and had the disability check sent directly to me. Now, I was responsible for paying my own bills. She also gave me the wheelchair ramps that had been custom built for her house so that I could get in and out of my own home easier.

My mother actually appeared happy for me during this time. She and I agreed that the scheduled appointment at Mary Free Bed was unnecessary. Neither of us attended.

Teens Making Adult Decisions

Robert and I were looking forward to our life together. Soon after school began, we made a decision to get pregnant. I was only sixteen years old. Robert's guidance counselor offered resources which led to me transferring to a closer school in Holland. This school assisted pregnant teenagers and the fathers of the babies to continue their education. It also had a nursery for the parents who needed childcare while they attended classes. At any time, without penalty, a mother or father was allowed to leave the classroom to be with their child.

Because we only had one vehicle during this time, Robert would catch the school bus, and I would drive myself to school. He remained at Saugatuck High School even though it was an option for him to join me. Nevertheless, Robert attended every appointment during my pregnancy, at times missing school. Ultimately, he quit the basketball team to work more hours.

As winter approached and I steadily gained weight, my back pain increased. It hurt before I became pregnant, but now it was constantly nagging. Using the wheelchair in the snow became a bit more difficult too. Later in my pregnancy, I struggled to balance on my left leg and lift my wheelchair in and out of the back seat of the car, but I was determined to remain independent.

We married when I was six months pregnant. Robert was eighteen and I was seventeen, young kids in love. We wanted to give our child something neither of us had, *married* biological parents. Robert and I had absolutely no guidance on what a healthy marriage looked like, but we were determined to do better than our parents. Although the order of my life was not biblical, I had a deep desire to please God and make Him happy with me. I knew that God saw everything, and I believed that He was pleased with our decision to marry.

Robert's father and my mother signed as witnesses on our marriage license at the Ottawa County District Courthouse. Robert and I had a memorable time on our honeymoon in Florida, going to Walt Disney World and Sea World. We returned home and continued to attend high school. Several weeks later my husband graduated earning his high school diploma. Both Robert and Albert were first-generation high school graduates. Considering our situation, it was quite an accomplishment and a joyful day to celebrate.

Before the sunrise one June day, my husband drove me to the hospital for an early morning cesarean section. The happiest moment of my life was seeing and holding our beloved son for the very first time. We named him Robert Allen, and he was the most precious gift and most beautiful part of my life.

I named him after his father and Rick Allen, the drummer from Def Leppard, solely because of the inspiration and hope he gave to me. I made a promise to my little guy that I was going to protect him and love him unconditionally. I knew the greatest gift was love, and I was excited to give him the love I never knew.

Although this was a preplanned procedure, I hemorrhaged greatly. I was anemic and initially refused a blood transfusion. Once I was told that my son would be discharged without me, and it may take over a month to recover, I agreed without delay and was immediately given four units of blood to replenish my body.

While I was in the hospital, between his work schedule and visiting us, my husband cleaned the entire trailer from top to bottom. Everything that was cleanable, he cleaned. My son and I were discharged on the fifth day. When we arrived home, it smelled fresh and everything was in place and organized. Could life get any better?

It was late August when I began my senior year in high school with my breastfeeding son by my side. My husband was working full-time, and I was genuinely happy.

Robert and I began discussing our future further and came to a decision that we needed a bigger home. Once again, I asked my mother to petition the court for money, and the judge allowed me to withdraw the remaining funds.

Robert and I purchased a brand-new double-wide manufactured home. The home was custom ordered to widen most doorways. While it was being constructed, we stayed with Robert's parents. Once the home was ready, it was placed in Maple Valley Estates located in Zeeland, Michigan. A very large carport was built over the main entrance deck and ramp. A second ramp was placed on the opposite side of the home as an emergency exit. Considering that Robert and I were still teenagers, we were doing well. We furnished our home and bought a second car. Life was perfect . . . or so it seemed.

It's strange how things can happen in life when everything seems so good. Just like in the garden of Eden, when everything was perfect and good, the snake slithered up to Eve and temptation made its deceitful appearance. One day you're enjoying peace, happiness, and contentment, then the next you find yourself bogged down with the heaviness of guilt, shame, and condemnation. That's the way sin works—it's insidious and crafty; its sole purpose is to steal, kill, and destroy whatever God considers good. Robert and I never saw it coming, but what happened next changed the direction of our lives forever.

Accident Photos

The lone tree stripped of bark revealed the impact of the accident.

Courtesy of Debra VanOrder, June 1987

After the impact, the 1985 four-door Chevrolet Chevette.

Courtesy of Debra VanOrder, June 1987

Hospitalization and Rehabilitation

Clinging to life following the accident.

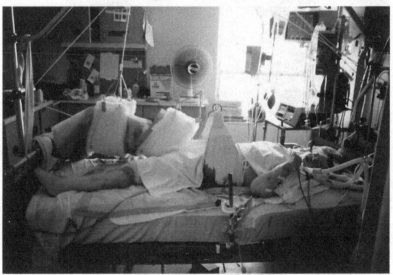

Tracy, at Butterworth Hospital, Intensive Care Unit, Grand Rapids, Michigan, June 1987
Courtesy of Debra VanOrder

Fractured and mangled from the waist down.
This was the last picture taken with my right leg.

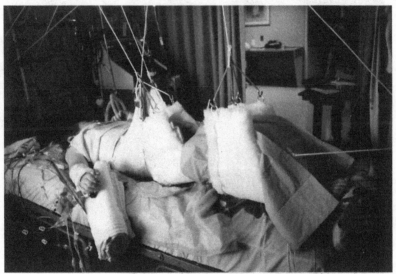

Tracy, at Butterworth Hospital, Intensive Care Unit, Grand Rapids,
Michigan, June 1987
Courtesy of Debra VanOrder

Right leg above the knee amputation with further injuries sustained.

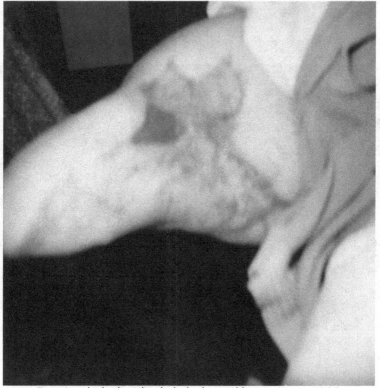

Tracy's right thigh, unhealed, discharged home. August 1988
Courtesy of Debra Causley

Left leg wound.

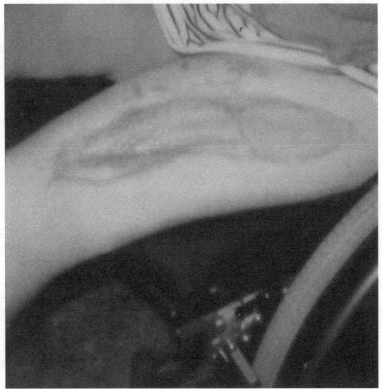

Tracy's left thigh, unhealed, discharged home. August 1988
Courtesy of Debra Causley

Smiling through the pain while standing with first prosthesis.

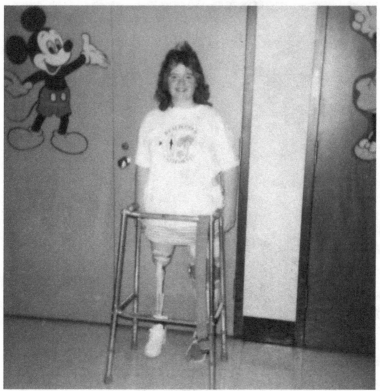

Tracy, at Mary Free Bed Rehabilitation Hospital, August 1988
Courtesy of Debra Causley

Plastic surgery, one of many.

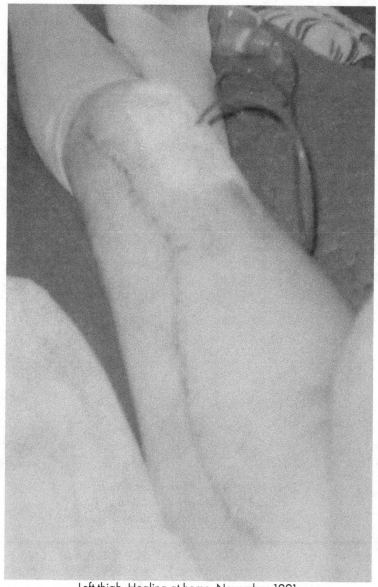

Left thigh. Healing at home. November 1991

My Son

Holding my beloved baby boy for the very first time after awakening from anesthesia.

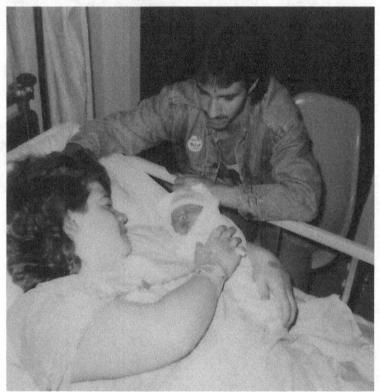

Tracy, Robert Allen, Robert Eugene Michaud
Holland Community Hospital, June 1990
Courtesy of Debra Causley

Praying God's perfect healing and protection over my son.

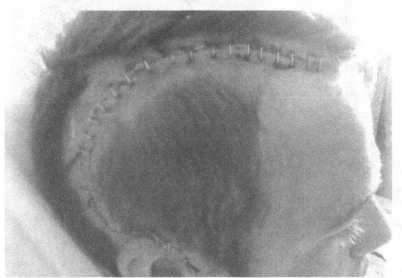

Robert Allen, two days after the removal of a benign meningioma tumor
Holland Community Hospital, June 2010
Courtesy of Robert Eugene Michaud

Mother-Son Dance.

Robert Allen and Tracy, The Barn at Monterey Valley, Allegan,
Michigan, June 2016
Courtesy of Chelsea Michaud

Mother-Son Dance.

Tracy and Robert Allen, The Barn at Monterey Valley, Allegan,
Michigan, June 2016
Courtesy of Chelsea Michaud

Celebrating with our son on his wedding day.

Albert, Tracy (Mother of the Groom), Robert Allen (Handsome Groom),
Robert Eugene (Father of the Groom)
The Barn at Monterey Valley, June 2016
Courtesy of Chelsea Michaud

My Family

Celebrating our mother's 52nd birthday.

Tracy, Debra, and Amy, our last photo together, December 2006
Courtesy of Debra Schoeneweis

Celebrating our new life in Christ.

Albert and Tracy, Baptisms in Lake Michigan, June 2010
(Not pictured: Robert Allen)
Courtesy of Chad Dykstra

Celebrating Mother's Day, a family filled with joy and new life in Christ.

Amy, Robert Eugene, Phyllis, Albert Sr., Albert, and Tracy
Third Coast Community Church, Saugatuck, Michigan, May 2017
Courtesy of Cara Williams

Amy's Hospitalizations

Sitting at my sister's bedside waiting for her to awaken
from a coma.

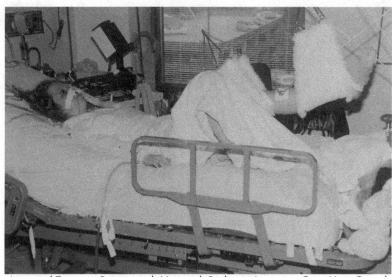

Amy and Tracy, at Butterworth Hospital, Pediatric Intensive Care Unit, Grand
Rapids, Michigan, May 1993
Courtesy of Debra Causley

Praying as I place my sister into God's hands.

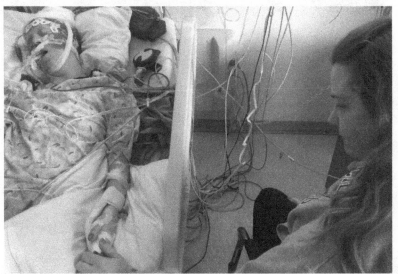

Amy and Tracy at Spectrum Health Butterworth Hospital, Intensive Care Unit,
Grand Rapids, Michigan, March 2017
Courtesy of Steffanie Vlasity

My Stepdaughters

Spending time together at a family karaoke party.

Jeanie and Tracy, our last picture together, August 2005
Courtesy of Albert Michaud

Celebrating with our daughter on her wedding day.

Tracy (Mother of the Bride) and Heather (Gorgeous Bride), Townline United
Methodist Church, Bloomingdale, Michigan, March 2015
Courtesy of Kate DeVries

Def Leppard - On Through the Years

The day when hope, inspiration, and encouragement changed my life.

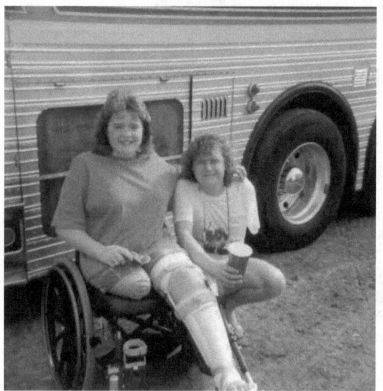

Tracy and Rick Allen, meeting for the first time, backstage at the Ionia Free Fair, Ionia, Michigan, August 1988
Courtesy of Anita Grant

Sharing accident stories.

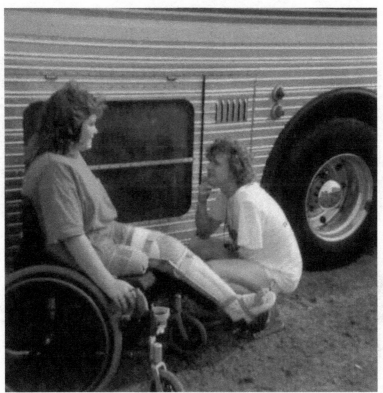

Tracy and Rick, at the Ionia Free Fair, Ionia, Michigan, August 1988
Courtesy of Anita Grant

Introducing my sister to Rick.

Tracy, Rick, and Amy
Jack Breslin Student Events Center, East Lansing, Michigan, December 1992
Courtesy of Def Leppard crew member

Introducing my son to Rick.

Robert, Rick, and Tracy
Van Andel Arena, Grand Rapids, Michigan, October 2005
Courtesy of Barb Kirby

Rick giving me permission to include him in this book.

Tracy and Rick
Comerica Park, Detroit, Michigan, July 2018
Courtesy of Heather Parks

CHAPTER 7

Unraveling Shame

Having the understanding darkened, being alienated from the life of God through the ignorance that is in them, because of the blindness of their heart.

Ephesians 4:18 (KJV)

LIFE WITH ROBERT AND THE BABY WAS WONDERFUL; IT WAS A LIFE I never knew could exist with happiness and family. The greatest joy I had was spending time with my husband and son. Little did I know the hopes and dreams I had envisioned for our future as a family would not even come close to being realized.

From the outside, one would never know how full of anguish my heart truly was, because when I was with my husband and son, I *was* happy. From the moment our eyes opened each day, Robert and I showered our son with attention and love. We poured into our son all that we had to offer, like we had promised to do. We desired to be the best parents possible, even enrolling in parenting classes held at a local church. Our son was our greatest love.

Education is extremely important to me; however, due to the accident, pregnancy, and demands of motherhood, I fell short of graduating with my class of 1991. I was disappointed that all my efforts, including two years of summer school, did not earn enough credits, but I was not going to allow that goal I failed to meet to discourage me. I was determined to finish my high school education one way or another. Life without a high school diploma would mean restricted job selection. I was already limited due to my disability. I had to press on. I was informed that I could still further my education with a GED certificate, so I went to the community education building in our county, took five examinations, and successfully passed each subject. From the beginning of the process until the end, it took several weeks. I then enrolled in college. I remember the day; it was not celebrated, but I couldn't have been more proud of myself. This was quite an accomplishment, considering all that had challenged me along the way. I had great self-satisfaction and was determined to succeed.

I attended college, but once my husband was hired full-time, I had to step away. Caring for my son was my utmost priority, and I just didn't trust anyone to care for him, apart from a few select family members. Coming from a background of abuse, I knew the risks. I promised him early on to protect him from perpetrators, a promise that drove many of my decisions both consciously and subconsciously.

Being a stay-at-home mom had many perks. Spending time with my son was the best part. I was able to maintain household chores, keep my home in tip-top condition, and spend more time with others, including my sister, Amy. She and I were very close. One day my sister and I were spending time together driving around. We were singing to our favorite music and eating our nachos and cheese from our regular stop at the Shell gas station when I noticed land for sale. This property was out in the country on a dead-end dirt road. Pine trees lined the front of the acreage. *I knew this was where I wanted to live.* I had lived in the city my entire life, and I was ready for a change. This was a perfect location. The property was nearly equal in distance from both our parents' homes. With my mother's guidance, my husband and I purchased the property and hired a contractor to begin preparations for our home to be relocated.

As happy as I was taking care of my son, the desire to earn a paycheck was strong, so I briefly worked at Burger King before applying at Teamwork, a temporary agency, landing a job working alongside my mother at Donnelly Mirrors. It was wonderful. I was making good money. My husband was home with our son during the day while I worked, and I was home with our son in the evening while he worked. We were apart a lot because of the work schedules, but we did not feel comfortable leaving our son in the care of anyone else. Robert and I were determined to protect our son and keep him safe. We had the best intentions as we placed our son first above all, but our marriage suffered greatly as a result. Life was still good, but it also left me vulnerable.

Months earlier, on an evening during the last weekend at our single-wide trailer, Albert and my half-brother came to visit. My son was at my mother's home overnight because Robert and I were finishing up the last bit of preparations before we moved out. The guys had an idea to get some beer, so we asked our neighbor, who was also a second cousin of mine, to purchase a case of beer. Without hesitation, he agreed. I drove Randy to Dunes View Kwik Shop. When I returned home, the guys decided they also wanted snacks. Robert and my brother drove back to the store. While they were gone, Albert dared me to "chug" a beer with him. I had never done that before. So I did. Not long after that, Albert leaned in for a kiss, a mutual kiss that changed everything.

From that moment, I rolled face first into a deep pit of guilt and shame that was too awful to acknowledge. What had I done? I was so ashamed. My feelings were beginning to increase for Albert as well. I shared this with both of my parents, hoping they could help me, but neither offered any advice or support, only their opinions. Their lack of guidance allowed me to move forward in this sin. I certainly didn't have good role models to rely on, and I knew nothing about marriage. At seventeen, I knew what was taking place was completely wrong and what I was feeling was wrong, but the need for acceptance and unconditional love was stronger as I felt love from both brothers. Robert provided peace, security, stability, and showered me with gifts, while Albert provided all the things mysterious and perverted, which I was also drawn to. And to be completely honest, Albert's longing to be with me and his pursuit of me despite our reality was exciting. It made me feel lovable, pursued, and wanted. As a teen, the only way I could describe them was one twin was good-hearted and the other not so much. There is so much more to each of them, but to give you a glimpse into my life at the moment, that would be a brief, naïve description. I turned to both of them to fill the void, the gaping hole that only God can fill. It was definitely a form of idolatry. As different as I describe them, they were inseparable, and when they were together, they enjoyed the same things, especially sports.

During a time when I should have been completely overjoyed, I was instead internally miserable. Guilt was my constant companion. I could not hold it in any longer. I told my husband what had taken place and promised I would never do it again. Miraculously, Robert forgave me and his brother, but not much time passed before Albert and I began having a full-blown affair which never ended. We lived a lie—a double life—for many, many years.

> *Come near to God and he will come near to you. Wash your hands, you sinners, and purify your hearts, you double-minded.*
>
> James 4:8

Hitting Bottom

Leading a double life happens more often than people would like to acknowledge. Whether it's the façade you put on before entering the church building, or the difference in your behavior at work versus at home, or your online presence versus your real life without filters, maybe a hidden pornography addiction or an affair—all of us wear a mask of some form. Living in a dual world of any circumstance is deception. Deception is sin. "If we claim to be without sin, we deceive ourselves and the truth is not in us" (1 John 1:8).

Albert longed for love, security, and acceptance. His parents did not provide these things for him and his brother. Unlike Robert, Albert did not make the resolve to change the generational sin nature that was clearly evident in their parents. Albert and his girlfriend were living with his parents; they already had a three-month-old daughter, Heather. As he watched those closest to him marry at a young age, he desired that too. So Albert married Heather's mother. Eight months later, Mary Jean "Jeanie" was born. But Albert's heart's desire was focused on me the entire time.

Even though Albert rented an apartment and moved his family in, still our affair continued. I decided to write him a note explaining how I felt and that we had to stop. *Physically* it did, briefly. Albert's drinking increased greatly, and he began another short-lived affair with his friend's wife. Selfishness was another generational theme his parents passed on, along with lack of discipline and consequences. Albert grew up watching every adult around him drink in excess. Albert followed in his parent's footsteps, day after day, as he drank his insecurities away. For him it was the natural thing to do. Albert was miserable. He left his wife and moved back in with his parents. They divorced and custody was granted 50/50 because the girls were so young and not yet in school. But a later incident had the Michigan State Police physically removing his daughters from their mother's home and literally dropping them off at his residence. Albert gained sole physical custody.

I don't know how I found myself intertwined with a man who himself was intertwined with sin. Yet after my promises to Robert about not falling into the same dysfunction as our parents, here I was. Albert's sin didn't just affect him; it affected me, his marriage, his daughters, his friendships—everyone in his life. And I was caught up in it. I had a deep sense that Albert was searching for love and acceptance like I was, but the way we acted upon trying to gain the things we desired—to heal the pain we both endured as children, the things only God could heal—were wrong.

Even though I was conflicted *daily*, I continued living in the dysfunction. My greatest fear was that if I told Robert once again about the affair, he would leave me and I would lose my son. My mother played into my fears by reminding me often that Robert would get custody of our son because I was disabled. Because I didn't know any better, I believed her. And I truly loved both brothers, to the extent that I knew what love was, anyway. I was constantly being tossed to and fro, torn between the brothers. I loved Albert's girls, too, and longed to help them in whatever way possible. I could not imagine my life without any of them. Music was *still my security, food still my comfort, and my son the only reason to persevere.* I could not live without my son, and I had absolutely no idea of how to do the right thing because I didn't know what the right thing was. My heart and my head were in a cyclone of disarray twenty-four hours a day. I knew I needed help, and I needed it fast.

Secretly, I began seeing a counselor. I needed assistance in regaining my inner peace. I could not just shake it off. The enemy doesn't want you to reveal the truth, because if it is brought out of the darkness and into the light, then the lies will be exposed and broken, and he will lose ground. The truth brings healing and wholeness, but the devil does all he can to keep us stuck in fear and shame. If only I had known then what I know now, I would have told the counselor everything, but fear and shame forced me to keep it inside. I was unable to tell the counselor exactly why I felt so terrible. He assumed it was because I was an amputee and had a horrible traumatic childhood. Sure, that was some of it, but it wasn't why I felt so awful. I kept my affair stuffed down and soon quit going to counseling altogether. My life unraveled even further.

An Appalling Proposition

My dad was a pervert. Anyone who was around him for more than a few minutes soon learned this, and chances are they would hear a dirty, dark joke, whether they wanted to or not. Many times, he laughed alone.

One afternoon while my husband was at work, my dad called. He invited me over to visit him while he was dog sitting for my grandmother. I decided to take my son over for a visit. When I arrived, I unloaded my wheelchair, wheeled around the car to open the passenger side door, and leaned into the back seat to unbuckle my son from his car seat. Then I held him securely while I sat down in the wheelchair and proceeded to alternate arms, holding him and propelling the wheelchair forward through the gravel driveway, through the grass, up to the cement in front of the house.

My dad opened the door to greet us. I was taken aback by his physical appearance. There he stood with an alcoholic beverage and cigarette in hand, wearing only a shirt, underwear, socks, and shoes. I was uncomfortable, but willingly rolled myself inside to the living room.

My dad made his way to the couch and sat in a way that was inappropriate. I was feeling more uneasy. Almost immediately after standing my son at the coffee table, he reached out to grab the only item on the table, a red box of condoms. I nervously laughed, and said, "No. You won't need those for a long time." My dad replied, "If my wife came here and saw you here and me in my underwear, she'd think we were having sex. So, why don't we?" I was shocked!

Immediately, I leaned forward and picked my son up and placed him on my lap. I was scared! Without hesitation, I began wheeling us out of that environment. I couldn't believe what was taking place. My dad said some horrific things to me as I was leaving. I absolutely did not deserve the abusive things that flew out of his mouth.

My heart was racing and pounding out of my chest. I hurried as fast as I could to place my son in his car seat, buckle him in, and wheel around my car to load my wheelchair into the back seat. I jumped in, started my car, and backed out of the driveway, vowing *never* to place myself or my son in harm's way. My biological father betrayed me in a way that I truly didn't think was possible. I was wrong. I shared with my mother what took place. She said, "That don't surprise me." I was broken. I wish I could say this was the lowest point in my life—the fact that my biological father had propositioned me for sex in front of my ten-month-old was appalling enough—but my need for approval and love from my mother led me down my darkest road yet.

Surrendered Secrets

If we confess our sins, he is faithful and just and will forgive us our sins and purify us from all unrighteousness.

1 John 1:9

For over two decades, I struggled with details of my past that so grieved God. I carried a burden and hid silent pain which left me exhausted, feeling worthless and unforgivable. I held on to undisclosed secrets that imprisoned me and kept me full of shame. I buried the memories so deep inside the recesses of my memory bank that, at times, I forgot. However, when the truth resurfaced, in various unhealthy ways, I numbed the pain.

A few select individuals knew about the affair and placed no judgment upon me. I knew God loved me, but I believed adultery and abortion was something He would not forgive, because I could not forgive myself. The lying, mind-binding spirits of unworthiness and shame followed me around like a dark, heavy rain cloud.

Since the car accident, my mother often talked about wanting another baby. She would also remind me of the reason why she was unable to conceive, referring to the hysterectomy she had to undergo in the early days of my hospitalization.

My mother blamed me and the stress related to the car accident for the reasons she had cervical cancer. I knew in my heart it had nothing to do with me. However, she would always utter, "If you would have listened to me and not driven, then . . ."

Despite her constant rejection and lack of affection toward me, I loved my mother more than anything. I was longing for her to love me in return the way that I loved her. One day while having a conversation with my husband, I asked him what he thought about my having a baby for my mother. We discussed it at length, knowing that it could be life-threatening for me as I hemorrhaged greatly with our son. After much discussion, we agreed; we were doing this for my mother only.

I presented the idea to my mother. She was overjoyed. I truly was not sure how she would react, but her face lit up. She was delighted and wanted to think about it.

A few weeks passed before she informed me of her decision, expressing how she was so happy to accept this gift of love. Completely unexpected, she offered to give us $25,000 but only after the baby was born. The money did not concern me. This was solely out of love for my mother.

I soon became pregnant. I shared the wonderful news with my mother. A few days later she invited me over to her home. I was not there long when she handed me an envelope with money inside. Before I could actually see how much money was in the envelope, she said, "It's for an abortion. I changed my mind." I was broken. I had no words. I did not know a thing about abortion.

I drove home and shared the news with my husband. We knew from the beginning this was exclusively for my mother, and no emotional attachment was established for either of us. My husband and I were perfectly content with having one child, our son.

My mother arranged to have her neighbor, who I knew as well, watch our son while my husband and I went to Grand Rapids for the appointment.

Afterward, although it was legal, my husband and I knew that what we had done was wrong. We agreed that we were going to keep this our secret, never telling anyone, especially our son, ever.

For me, just nineteen years old, shame set in all the more, as well as anger toward my mother. Within months, my husband underwent a vasectomy. Together we made a decision that would be permanent, that we believed was the best, considering our situation, not knowing how it would ultimately affect us in the future.

My life was a mess, and I was miserable. I was an unfaithful wife. My brother-in-law, Albert, knew *all of my secrets*. He was *one* of them. I ended up having a few one-nighters too, but Albert was the one I regularly had unprotected sex with. I was so lost, broken, and depressed. Two years passed, and again I was pregnant. Nothing can stay hidden forever. "You may be sure that your sin will find you out" (Numbers 32:23). There's an old saying: you are only as sick as your secrets. Secrets are meant to come out so you may be free and healed of them. But panicked over my pregnancy, in secrecy and out of desperation, I again chose what seemed like the only option—abortion.

This is what sin does when we do not flee temptation by taking every thought captive. Temptation begins with a thought in our minds, and if you think about it long enough, you will cave. Whether it's a candy bar, an extra-long gaze upon someone's body, or a click on a picture or link, sin is there, lurking. Sin—whether it's gluttony, lust, or perversion, whatever the sin—will eventually be exposed. Sin is serious. It's been said, "Sin will take you farther than you want to go, keep you longer than you want to stay, and cost you more than you want to pay." Sin is costly. Romans 6:23 tells us, "For the wages of sin is death." I knew my life was a disaster and I was headed for a great fall into a pit of utter devastation.

I was blind, deceived, and truly unaware of how completely detached I was from reality. I had hit rock bottom, the bottom of a pit that I never wanted to be in.

I listened to music all the time and cried often. I wrote the following during the darkest days I struggled through.

> Life to me seems to be an unconquerable mission. No matter what one accomplishes, it never seems to be enough. Unsatisfied, one keeps searching for new ways to find happiness and satisfaction within oneself, realizing it's an endless, very depressing, unrealistic goal to achieve. One can pretend to "be there" now. But in one's own visualization of self-image, every hope and realistic dream fades to black, realizing one is just existing, not living. As days and time go by, one wishes they could stop the world and catch up and live free. That would be true, honest life to me! Believing. Hoping is the key to succeeding!

Life from the Bottom of the Pit

Friday, May 21, 1993, was a day that is forever etched into my memory. Just shy of my six-year anniversary of my accident, my sister was also involved in an accident. Amy was unresponsive and in critical condition. For the next twenty-one days, my sister remained in a coma. Time. Stood. Still. But my mind raced back and forth. I could not lose my sister! I remained at the hospital by her side.

One day, she finally "woke up." God sustained her, and I was grateful. He saved us both at the age of fourteen from tragic accidents. I was convinced that God had a purpose for us, but I had no idea what that truly looked like. Amy and I always had a saying that "Everything happens for a reason. Only God knows why."

The brain injury altered my sister's personality. This concerned me greatly because she, too, knew all of my secrets, and now she didn't have a filter, meaning she didn't think before she spoke. I was afraid she would blurt out my private conversations that I had with her, exposing my hidden sin and forcing me into a position that I was not prepared to be in. Thankfully, she never did. It was later determined that Amy was also completely blind in her right eye due to the trauma sustained. She had to relearn how to talk, walk, and be social. She was emotional, angry, and violent toward staff.

I made sure Amy had a radio. Music always brought us joy. I purchased a cassette single for my sister, a song by Whitney Houston called, "I Have Nothing Without You." I brought it up to Amy to play. While I was preparing to put the cassette in the player, another song came on the radio. To my surprise, Amy began singing as loud as she could with a hoarse voice, word for word to the song by Joe Cocker, "You Are So Beautiful." She looked directly at me and sang her heart out. I knew my sister was going to be okay.

It reminded me of a happier time before Amy's accident, when I was listening to the radio and the DJ announced they were giving away Def Leppard tickets. I got chills and decided to call the station to give it a shot. And lo and behold, I was the winner. I was beyond thrilled. I invited Amy to go with me to Kellogg Arena.

I picked Amy up, and we drove to Battle Creek. We arrived early in hopes that I could talk to the band's tour manager. We connected. For me, it was a joyful reunion in the midst of my life circumstances. I was so full of peace at the concert, while in the rest of my life, aside from my son, I felt so lost. Def Leppard music brought me unspeakable joy, and I felt special because of our connection. A few weeks later, a FedEx envelope arrived at my mother's home, my last known address to the band's tour manager. He wrote to me and sent some Def Leppard memorabilia.

Eleven weeks after the accident, Amy was discharged home. She was isolated to the beautifully remodeled basement. As Amy regained some normalcy in her life with new limitations, our stepfather began verbally abusing her. He would regularly call her a *one-eyed mental* and, once again, our mother did not step in to protect. She stood by her man, dysfunctional as he was, over her children who just wanted their mom.

Sadly, Amy followed in our mother's footsteps, allowing abuse to be at the center of her relationships. I did not know how to help her. I just knew I had to protect her whatever the cost.

Despite these very difficult circumstances, I had many things going well for me, but so many things going wrong too. I was doing everything I could to have some sense of normalcy, one way or another. Once my sister returned to school, our mother "hired" me to be Amy's transportation. I enjoyed driving her to and from school. I even got to attend two more Def Leppard concerts. One a few months after her accident, the other the next day in a neighboring city. The band was so sad to hear about Amy that they graciously signed memorabilia and wished her well. I couldn't get enough. Many years later, on separate occasions, I introduced Rick Allen to my son, Rob, and my stepdaughter, Heather.

My husband and I had a little bit of time in between the site preparations on our property and moving the double-wide from the mobile home park in Zeeland. After a few weeks of living with his parents, we were able to move back into our home, which was now located on four acres in the Saugatuck Public School district. I was filled with joy, yet full of pain, sadness, and hopelessness too. Only weeks after being back in our home, I underwent an abdominoplasty to get rid of the pouch over my cesarean scar. A few days later, I turned twenty-one. I knew I wasn't having the surgery for health reasons; it was to help me accept myself. I had myself convinced that *if only* the pouch was gone, I would try to walk with a prosthetic leg. And maybe, just maybe, my life would all work out and I wouldn't be in the mess that I was in. I was deceived. Living a double life will do this to you.

My life was more out of control than ever. Each morning I awoke to my husband and son. I would make us breakfast, and we would enjoy our time together. When my husband left for work, my son and I headed over to my in-laws' home where Albert and his girls lived. Our kids would play, Albert and I would enjoy our time together, and the regular drinking time would begin for the in-laws.

Albert, too, was drinking a case of beer by himself and soon lost his driver's license due to drinking and driving. Now he was required to attend MADD meetings and AA meetings. I took it upon myself to drive him back and forth to the meetings. No one else was financially able, and I was concerned for the girls' future.

I knew this was not the life I wanted for myself or for my son to be brought up in. I knew change had to happen; I just didn't know how to get there.

Upon enrolling my son in preschool, I began to volunteer, vowing to be supportive and help other children learn about disability. Robert and I were involved parents. We made ourselves available for the classroom or field trips as able.

I had a great desire to be financially independent and off of disability. I began seeking work while my son was in school. After applying to fifty-two different companies in three counties, with no success, I applied to Michigan Rehabilitation Services. Soon after, I had an interview with Thermotron Industries. I was hired. This was a sit-down position. I learned to assemble circuit boards for test chambers. From start to finish, I learned and enjoyed each task, but the job was demanding. On a few occasions my wheelchair tires went flat due to running over metal shavings; I even had a few that stuck in my pants, poking into my thighs which I did not feel. This was definitely a dangerous and eye-opening thing to find.

Although it was a sit-down position, there was a lot of physical lifting and bending and leaning over the line to work on the boards all day long. My back pain was increasing, but I kept ignoring it. I was so torn in life. I didn't know what to do. I had financial independence, but I was still miserable. I didn't feel I had any options because my mother reminded me often that I would lose my son if Robert and I didn't stay together. I began to accept this was the way my life was going to continue, and I had no one to blame but myself. When home, I would crank up the stereo and go outside and lay on our trampoline. Not a day or moment passed that I was not overwhelmed. I spent many evenings with my son, watching movies and eating our favorite snacks.

One day, I learned that my company would reimburse college students' financial expenses depending on the grade earned. An A would get 100 percent reimbursed, a B would get 75 percent, etc. I was excited. I had hope. I was now working full-time and began attending evening classes at Grand Rapids Community College. In the face of my circumstances, and despite the misery, I was determined to persevere and crawl out of the pit.

Decision Time

Over the course of several years, the dysfunction and double life continued. As a family, including Albert and the girls, we often attended a variety of outings, including monster truck shows, car races, and many others. I paid using my credit card. Life continued.

Albert regained his driver's license and completely quit drinking alcohol, breaking the generational sin pattern from both sides of his family. He knew drinking is one thing I would never accept "if" we were together. Albert was in love with me and wanted to be with me at all times, but it was such a difficult situation.

Albert decided to buy a home near us. One problem he encountered when applying was he needed a cosigner. Without my husband's permission, I cosigned.

Albert and his girls moved to Bravo. My son and I visited them many nights of the week, while my husband worked.

Despite the dysfunction, our kids were happy. I applied for a new position in my company and was promoted to marketing secretary. I really enjoyed my job, and college was going well.

My husband was promoted at work and had an upcoming conference to attend in Las Vegas for his job.

While he was away, Albert and I were together. We shared with each other how much we loved one another and talked about what would happen "if" the two of us were to get together. Albert said, "I don't care what others think," but I was scared and full of fear. I had deep love for my husband. He is a wonderful person, husband, father, friend, and provider. He did nothing to me to deserve how we had disrespected him. For that, I was so truly sorry. I cried at the thought of my behavior through the years. For me to live with myself, even though it wasn't a godly choice, I had to begin over and be totally honest, not only with myself, but with my husband. He deserved the truth. And it was the only way I could move forward toward healing. Upon my husband's return, I was emotionally detached, and he recognized it.

My husband asked his brother to watch our dogs because he was taking our family to Mackinac Island for a vacation. I was so very confused. I had so much guilt that I did not enjoy anything. All I could think about was Albert. It was decision time. When we returned home to pick up our dogs, Albert told me it was time for me to make a decision. He told me that he loved me and could not share me any longer. Lord, help me.

I talked with my husband and told him that I wanted a divorce. Initially, he didn't believe me and tried to convince me to remain in our home. I told Robert that I would let him have everything: our house, our dogs, whatever he wanted, but not our son. I could not live this dysfunctional way of life any longer. I had to just get out. I was so miserable trying to be "happy" in my situation of juggling my husband and his twin and what I should and should not do.

As if circumstances couldn't get any worse, I was addicted to over-the-counter ephedrine pills, which my dad had introduced me to. I began binge eating, dieting, and exercising, my life spiraling a little bit more out of control.

Robert and I talked extensively and discussed thoroughly how we would continue to raise our son. I was grateful that I had a son with him. He is a dedicated man, fully involved in his child's life. We promised to do what was best for our son, at all times, no matter what. New Year's Eve, we took off our wedding rings. Robert went to bed, and I went over to Albert's to begin the new decade with him. You see, unbridled freedom creates crisis. When there is no moral compass, you start to believe the lie that God is angry enough with us that He'll never be willing to forgive. That's a great deception, a lie Satan uses to keep us moving forward in sin and degradation. My heart became hardened, as I allowed the worldly ways of living to crowd out my conscience. I grieved the Holy Spirit each time I chose to ignore His convictions. My own choices created many self-defeating consequences as I settled for a dysfunctional lifestyle of chaos and pain.

I was a hot mess but always had a smile on my face. No one knew the depth of my pain and shame. But God did. I had no idea how God was going to work in all of this. I knew He loved me, but would He ever forgive me? The next ten years would be filled with a series of events that would bring Albert and me to our knees.

I will bring the blind by a way they did not know;
I will lead them in paths they have not known.
I will make darkness light before them,
and crooked places straight.
These things I will do for them,
and not forsake them.

Isaiah 42:16 (NKJV)

CHAPTER 8

Set Aside to Be Set Apart

God grant me
the serenity to accept
the things I cannot change,
courage to change
the things I can,
and the wisdom to
know the difference.

Reinhold Niebuhr (1951)[3]

As THE YEAR 2000 APPROACHED, THE WORLD WAS FILLED WITH anxiety due to the so-called "Millennium Bug." There was speculation that the turn of the century would confuse and shut down computer systems, causing utter devastation around the globe. It was said the impact could affect mortgage fees at the banks, cause power plants to malfunction, interfere with our airlines, you name it—if it was computer-related, there was cause for alarm. Some people believed it was a hoax, while others believed the world was going to end. But as you can see, the world kept turning.

Amid all the chaos, my life went on. Albert and I were hoping once we lived together that everything would fall into place and we would live happily ever after. He was content. I was not. One reason was because his home was not fully accessible. Daily I had to navigate a step with my wheelchair to enter the kitchen or bathroom. Initially this was not a concern of mine because we just wanted to be together, but when it became a repeated occurrence throughout the day, it was demanding and strenuous on my shoulders.

I was working full-time and attending college several evenings a week. I had already initiated a divorce with Robert, and he remained in our home with our son for a few months. Then my son moved in with Albert, the girls, and me. Albert transferred his girls, Heather and Jeanie, to the school where my son attended. Due to Jeanie's medical history, I informed the staff of her inhaler protocol, ensuring she was able to keep it with her at all times. I was involved in the kids' schooling, making sure homework was finished and turned in on time, and I volunteered as I was able and attended parent-teacher conferences. For the girls, I went with Albert. For my son, I went with Robert. At every encounter, I was weighed down with a blanket of guilt and shame. I knew my life was a mess, but I was willing to endure the whispers of judgment because I genuinely loved Albert, and especially our sex life.

Sex had become an idol for both of us. We were perverse as taught by our perpetrators. Worldly pleasure was an idol for us, including pornography and strip clubs. Looking back, that was one of the lowest times of my life. But at the time, I saw it as pleasure. Albert and I very much enjoyed our lifestyle together, or at least we thought we did. We later learned that's not what the other truly wanted. We both did those things assuming that's what the other wanted, when in fact, we just wanted each other.

Aside from God, Albert was the only one who knew *everything* about me and loved me unconditionally. I was his everything, and he was mine. Albert regularly reminds me that from the moment we met as kids, he knew I was the one. He once wrote me a letter saying, "The way you make me feel is indescribable. I could never trust or love another the way I do you." I know he has always loved me—I just wish things had been different from the start. We could have avoided so much pain between Robert and me and our families, but Albert wasn't the man I needed at that time, and besides, I wouldn't have had my son, who means everything to me.

God knew exactly what we were doing, and I knew that; it was time to make things right. I didn't want to live this way any longer—I wanted to do it God's way and begin a new life that was no longer living in sin. Albert and I got married, though we were too poor to buy each other wedding rings. I needed his healthcare coverage and the timing seemed right, even though we didn't have a stable plan. I felt God was pleased. I was no longer living in sin. So far, this new decade was delivering more than I had hoped for, but the heavy weight of guilt was ever so present. Two weeks after we married, Albert's parents got married after nearly four decades of living in sin. To me, this was clear evidence that generational sin was being broken, which maybe was God's plan all along. When we begin to honor God in the things that matter to Him, people and lives change for the better. And others notice.

Unworthy and Unforgivable

With our marriage came some interesting consequences. For starters, my son is biologically my husband's nephew, but now his uncle is his stepfather. The kiddos are legally first cousins, but because their fathers are identical twins, at the DNA level, they are biologically half-siblings. I had *always* wondered how our children would explain this if they were ever asked. How would their future spouses react? Would Albert and I be embraced or rejected? What about their weddings? On and on my thoughts went. I was internally miserable, and Psalm 51:3 reminded me, "My sin is always before me." Yep. As I went about each day with a smile on my face, I still had a heavy heart, and the constant dialogue played in my head.

For way too long Satan smothered me with the lies that I was unworthy and unforgivable, that I deserved to live the rest of my life in misery based on the poor decisions I had made in my teens and twenties. And when Albert and I endured a miscarriage four months into pregnancy, those lies built strongholds in my mind that I—we—deserved this because Galatians 6:7 says we reap what we sow. I ended up getting a tubal ligation to save myself more misery later on. These kinds of wrong-thinking patterns affected my life for years to come.

I often told myself that if the Michaud family ever disowned me, at least I would have my son.

I began searching the Scriptures for advice and answers. I desperately desired God to give me peace. I wanted to learn what a godly wife looked like, what a godly husband looked like, what a godly marriage consisted of because Albert and I did not have any good or godly role models to learn from. As I focused on Psalm 51:1–12, I cried and begged God to "have mercy on me . . . blot out my transgressions . . . let the bones you have crushed rejoice." I felt the heavy cloud of desperation slowly dissipate. I felt God's presence and believed He was going to restore me and bring joy back into my life. I just felt lighter and somehow knew God was going to sustain me.

Things continued to get harder. Albert's employer of nine-plus years closed. Eventually, he was hired at a company in Holland. Then, when we had been married for only three months, still with no wedding rings to symbolize our commitment, Albert lied to me. This particular day, I brought Albert lunch. He ate it quickly, and a few minutes later he said, "Well, I am going to get going now." We kissed, and I told him I'd see him later. As I drove out of the parking lot, I turned at the stop sign and looked to my left, and I watched Albert get into the back seat of a four-door car with a few women he worked with. Albert had promised me that he wouldn't smoke marijuana with them anymore.

Statistically, I knew the odds were stacked against us from the get-go, but our dysfunction added to that exponentially. We had always promised to be honest with each other, although we had not been in previous relationships. I lost a lot of confidence that he would tell me the truth after that. So, I gave him a choice—me or his job. He chose me. I had never expected to give an ultimatum like this. I was emotional not only because *he chose me,* but because he loved me so deeply. At this point, I knew we would get through anything together.

Albert and I did our best to pay bills with my disability check, but it was not enough. Utility bills were coming in with shut-off notices. My husband procrastinated in looking for work, and he would not seek outside help. It was hard to put food on our table, so I went to a local church and received food assistance and resources for our family. Somebody had to do something, and I guess that somebody was me.

At a time when Albert and I had no business leaving Michigan, we graciously accepted an opportunity to escape the winter weather and enjoy a free getaway at a condo on the shores of the Atlantic in Daytona Beach. What was supposed to be a relaxing and refreshing time of renewal, taking in the glorious sunrises and soaking up the warmth before Albert's job search, turned into a nightmare.

One evening, after we had a few alcoholic beverages, I injured myself. Afterward, I was unable to move my residual limb without restriction and pain. Although I didn't realize the extent of the damage, I did notice bruising. A few days after we arrived home, I was still experiencing pain. My husband drove me to the hospital. X-rays revealed I had broken my right hip. I was admitted to the hospital and had surgery the following day to reposition the bones and insert pins and screws to hold the bones together to heal properly.

It was shortly after fracturing my right hip that I heard God speak to me. I knew that I knew it was Him. I so longed for everything to be all right. Although treatment for my osteoporosis would not come until a few years later, the fracture was a clear result of my sedentary lifestyle. During this time of healing and physical therapy, I fully relied on my husband to care for me, but God had my full attention. I clearly heard Him say to me, "*I am allowing you and Albert to be together, but it's not going to be easy.*" I shared that with my husband. We knew something had to change. Albert and I repented. This was a turning point in our lives, one where generational sin was being broken and our lives went from hopeless to hopeful.

If My people who are called by My name will humble themselves,
and pray and seek My face,
and turn from their wicked ways,
then I will hear from heaven,
and will forgive their sin and heal their land.

2 Chronicles 7:14 (NKJV)

My biological father reentered my life but not without me setting some *very* clear boundaries for myself and the children. He helped us out and encouraged Albert to get his CDL. As a desperate measure, my husband applied and was hired for a trucking job, which left me home with the kids for two weeks at a time. The parenting exchanges between the girls' mother and stepfather and me became heated. We had peace officers attend exchanges. I told Albert I didn't want to be involved in the exchanges any longer. He needed to be present. Albert and I discussed our situation.

We believed our love would lead to happiness one day. We knew that we were unable to care for our children financially at this point. We offered the other parents the chance to raise them. They accepted. Albert and I lost our kids because of our own selfish desires and many poor choices along the way. This was another defining moment in our lives. It was truly humbling to admit that our life choices had finally caught up with us. We were unable to hold together all that we worked so hard to achieve.

Albert and I knew God was nearby, though, and we made a promise to each other before Him to do what was right to the best of our abilities, but this was a very, very hard time of sadness and grief as our family unit was no more.

All we ever knew was falling apart. Each day I awoke, I thanked God for the strength He gave us to endure. But I was so filled with guilt. Life became dreadful.

Albert and I moved in with his parents because we had two mortgages. Robert had moved. Our goal was to move back into my home once we were financially able. We sold Albert's home and paid down some debt. But in the meantime, our living space was *upstairs*. I had to use my forearm crutches to get up the stairs, and I used my wheelchair when downstairs. It was physically taxing on my entire body. I just settled into the life I was a part of while Albert was on the road.

With Albert gone so much, I missed him greatly. He wrote me letters while on the road. I responded in writing, but he was only able to read them when he arrived home. We talked on the phone as much as we were able to connect. We did not have cell phones back then, so it was hit and miss. The distance was getting to us.

We decided for a very brief time for me to go on the road with him. Picture this: me, using crutches to walk through truck parking lots in changing weather climates and climbing in and out of a semi tractor. It was physically exhausting! We had two little dogs with us, and between Albert, them, and me all riding in the cab of the truck, it was difficult, to say the least, especially when it came time for them to go potty. As most people know, truckers get paid by the mile, so time on the road equals money, and frequent stops mean slow progress. But I loved the view. I loved the peace. No collection-agency calls. It was a short season for me but not for Albert.

This went on for two months. The days were long, and we were only able to see our kids every other weekend. I was so depressed that I stopped going on the road and moved back into my home with our dogs. Almost immediately, my son moved back, and Jeanie did as well. My oldest stepdaughter remained with her mother. Albert continued to write to me while he was on the road. He often reassured me that he would never hurt me, and that someday I would truly believe that. I was a hot mess. But finally, after nineteen months of being married, we had enough money saved to purchase our wedding rings. What a joyful day!

Albert finished the year-long contract and then quit so he could be home. He was not able to find long-term employment in the area. Once again, we returned to living off of my disability check. I applied at the school for free/reduced breakfasts and lunches for the kids. We were able to once again get food assistance. I began taking the kids to Matthew 25 Ministries, one of the resources we were given to find items we needed. I was grateful and humbled by the generosity of the people who donated for individuals like us in need, which gave me a deep desire to want to assist others in his or her time of need as well. I soon began volunteering on a weekly basis. I loved helping the people. I felt a glimmer of hope again.

Joy and Pain in the Mundane

Life went on as usual. All the while I felt ashamed of myself for not working or going to school. I mean, what kind of role model is that?! My son was involved in many sports. His father and I attended his home and away games together. We also attended banquets together. Robert rode along with me and assisted with getting my wheelchair in and out of the car. We listened to music, sang, and talked. As much as I knew he and I were friends and supporting our son without the Friend of the Court involved, I felt guilty. I was truly sorry for my selfishness in giving into temptation and having an affair. I apologized to Robert many times, and he has always forgiven me. I just couldn't seem to forgive myself. I literally *lived* for my son. My goal was to see him graduate. If I made it to that point, I would be okay to die because that is how much daily misery accompanied me, including great physical pain.

I had already quit working and attending college, so I was able to resume Jeanie's medical care because her mother did not participate and really did not believe she was even sick. Albert and the girls' mother continued fighting in court. Albert and I argued over our situation. It felt hopeless.

I continued to visit my sister while she spiraled out of control with her drinking. Many times I assisted her, but her abusive, codependent relationship with her boyfriend was the only love she knew. It was awful. My heart was heavy for my sister all the time. I also became my mother-in-law's caregiver, taking her to and from doctor's appointments. At age fifty-seven, she quit drinking and smoking.

One day in early September, I went to a yard sale at a house in Holland. It happened to be the house I lived in when my stepfather began molesting me. It was the home that my mother partied in and played with the Ouija board as a teenager. It was the home that brought me great joy in remembrance of listening to my mother's albums and singing along, but also the home of deep, painful memories. I bought a few things, then asked the people if I could go inside. I told them I was raised there for a few years. Using my forearm crutches, as I regularly did in environments that were not wheelchair accessible, I carefully walked around the house, balancing on my left leg.

Everything was as I remembered. As I opened the basement door, I was expecting the damp, musky odor to fill my nostrils with pain and sadness, but what a joyful surprise! I smelled puppies. The *only* smell that came up the stairs at me was the smell of puppies. Newborn puppies. Just as it was when I was six years and younger. It was such a good memory. One of very few. I left there with a renewed sense of peace that was unexpected and indescribable. For some reason, I felt a deep sense of God's presence reminding me that He was with me and everything was going to be okay.

As I drove home, I had an unexplainable urge to go somewhere. A spontaneous adventure. I evaluated our vehicle situation, and before I knew it, I was packed up with the kids and headed to Vegas. You see, my mother promised me when I was an inpatient in the hospital that she would take me to Vegas. She never did. I became bitter toward her, because to me it was just another broken promise. I had made the same promise to my kids, and I didn't want my kids to feel the same way about me. I wanted my word to mean something, to be trustworthy to my kids. We went for it and made it there and back in a week, with a lot of funny, sad, trying, scary, and memorable moments. I cried a lot too. I learned not to make any more promises and to be a person of my word, that it's important to let my yes be yes and my no be no.

Although my family didn't get to see or do a thing aside from swimming in the hotel pool in the dry heat, a promise was fulfilled. *Thank you, Lord Jesus, for protecting us and allowing me to take my kids there,* because unbeknownst to us, something tragic was in store for us a year later.

Choosing Life

Our arrival home from Las Vegas was filled with creditors constantly calling. Albert dealt with them and worked out payment arrangements. While the kids were in school, we gathered belongings of value and pawned them for necessities. We were at a really low point.

I was depressed, and my physical pain was so great that I laid down frequently. It's been said that physical pain and depression are closely intertwined—one can cause the other and so forth. It's a continuous, vicious cycle, like an out-of-control merry-go-round I just could not get off. I contacted my original physician at Mary Free Bed Rehabilitation Hospital. He referred me to another physician for an evaluation and counseling. I was going to have to wait several weeks. Months later, I was seen by a psychiatrist, and although I did not share many personal details about my life, I did talk about my childhood, the car accident, and my mother. He said I had a mood disorder, bipolar II, prior to the accident. Eventually, the doctor prescribed mood-stabilizing medication, which I gladly accepted. I was desperate and willing to take *anything* to feel better. He consulted with my physician at Mary Free Bed to have a home evaluation.

In the meantime, I was still in a tremendous amount of pain. Albert felt helpless, and it hurt him seeing me like that. We were desperate. He knew a man since childhood who we visited one evening, and he offered me morphine. The man put some liquid drops into my glass of pop, and I drank it. Not much time went by. I could not feel any pain. My pain was gone, but I was a bit out of it. The man offered to sell us the bottle for fifty dollars. We agreed.

I would take that morphine immediately after the kids got on the school bus. I wasn't sure how much I needed, but I did what I saw the man do. A few days had gone by, and I clearly remember hearing the words, "*Get up or you're going to die.*" I lay on my bed looking straight down at the carpet wondering what had happened to me. I realized this was God's message to me. He had saved my life again. I told Albert what I heard, and he went directly to the bathroom cabinet and emptied the morphine bottle. Sometimes we'll do anything to ease our pain, whether it's emotional or physical. The things of the world promise to give us an easy way out, but it only leads to devastation.

When I had regained some of my strength, I got up and went out to the living room and turned on our television. We only were able to receive a few channels with the speaker wire stapled across the ceiling for reception. I stopped on a program called *Enjoying Everyday Life*. I do not recall the message, but I did verbally recite the sinner's prayer at the end of the program. At this point, I only knew that I was not going to hell when I died. I had a strong desire to learn more. I faithfully watched Joyce Meyer and began to feel a glimmer of hope again.

As I heard one teaching after another, day after day, things began to change. For one thing, Albert and I stopped hanging around certain individuals, including some family members. We noticed that our desire for worldly pleasure diminished tremendously, and we were swearing less. Albert and I began to consider our part in each trial we had endured, and we radically changed our behavior. Those closest to us didn't understand what we were doing, but we did not care. We were determined to do the right thing because we had done it wrong for way too long. In John 14:6 Jesus says, "I am the way and the truth and the life." Albert and I desired to have the life He offered. We chose to follow Jesus.

Blessings Begin

Our holidays that year were definitely memorable. Although the weather conditions did not allow us to pick up our daughter, Heather, we were grateful for the Thanksgiving food box provided by the local church. Upon pick up, they also requested clothing sizes for each of us for Christmas. I was humbled, stunned by the generosity of complete strangers.

Christmas that year was not going to be about gifts. It was going to be *all about Jesus*. Albert and I had absolutely no money, yet Rob and Jeanie were insistent upon us having a real Christmas tree. While my husband and I were in the house, the kids went outside. A bit of time passed, and the kids knocked on the sliding glass door. They had brought us a tree. Rob and Jeanie had climbed one of our pine trees with hand saws and cut down the top! After my mind raced back and forth of all that could have gone wrong while they were up there, I was overjoyed by their persistence. They brought the tree inside and decorated it with what ornaments and lights they could find out in our shed. We did end up purchasing each of the kids a fifty-cent gift because that was all we could gather. Our family was blessed once more by the local church with a gift bag for each family member. Our Christmas was truly blessed.

As I continued to draw near to God, He used Psalm 91:1–2 to show me that He would be my refuge as I rested in Him. It was when I decided to fully trust the Lord that the stability and security I had always craved began to show up in my life. As Albert and I walked with God and learned from Him, we began to receive one blessing after another. We realized and fully understood that it was God's goodness, grace, and mercy that were manifesting material blessings and showing up in relationships. God had forgiven us. As we received God's forgiveness, we extended forgiveness to those in our lives also. Forgiveness is an ongoing process, but as we walk in love and forgiveness, continual blessings abound. As Albert and I look back on this time in our lives, we recognize that it was solely the Lord who sustained us. He has said, in Hebrews 13:5, "Never will I leave you." Albert and I are stronger individuals as a result of God's unconditional love and protection.

When you seek God and walk with Him, you can experience this too. The peace, joy, security, and blessings that He provides for me, He will provide for you too. He was there for me; He'll be there for you too. God loves us all so much that He sent His Son to die for us.

How could I get my family to see the truth I had come to know? Could I love *my* family at all cost? Would I lose my mind? Would I lose my health? Would I lose my life? These were questions I wrestled with daily. Fortunately, He knew the answers.

CHAPTER 9

Live to Give

A new commandment I give to you, that you love one another; as I have loved you,
that you also love one another. By this all will know that you are My disciples, if you
have love for one another.

John 13:34–35 (NKJV)

IN ANY RELATIONSHIP, STRUGGLES ARE REAL AND EXPECTED, BUT WITH
God at the center of your life, He gives you the strength to love the
unlovely, the hard people in your life, including difficult family
members. Things continued to decline for our family, financially and
physically; I guess sometimes things get worse before they get better. I
met with a bankruptcy lawyer to discuss my options, while my husband
gained temporary employment as a delivery driver around West
Michigan. I still had not forgiven myself for all the poor choices I had
made, and it was beginning to take a toll. I was spiritually oppressed.
Looking back, knowing what I know now, it was clear I was in the
middle of a spiritual battle, and the devil was doing all he could to keep
me from moving forward. My mother was ill. My stepdaughter was ill.
My sister was ill. Even my healthy, teenage son started experiencing
health issues. Everyone seemed to need me, but I wasn't whole myself.
There were some very challenging times ahead of us, but somehow I
was able to focus more of my energies on helping others, assisting them
in their time of need. This next season of our lives was full of appointments, physical exhaustion, and uncertainty, but in the middle of it,
God used our family in ways we could never have imagined.

Jeanie's Story

From birth, Albert's daughter, Jeanie, was quite sick. She'd had multiple medical appointments and was placed on numerous antibiotics and medications. She had a persistent cough, and her nose was always crusted over. Jeanie was diagnosed as having idiopathic thrombocytopenic purpura (ITP), a blood disorder, meaning she was prone to excessive bleeding and bruising because her platelets were so low. She was also diagnosed with asthma and given various medications, including steroids and several inhalers. For six years, Albert and I regularly brought Jeanie to see a pulmonologist. We could not understand how she and my mother, who had lung cancer, could be on the exact same inhaler for breathing issues. Albert and I pushed to get Jeanie evaluated at Helen DeVos Children's Hospital. We were waiting on a follow-up return visit.

The phone rang. It was the girls' mother. Jeanie was on a bimonthly weekend visit and was supposed to return home that evening. The ER physician instructed Jeanie's mother to call and inform Albert that Jeanie was in the emergency room. That morning her sister, Heather, was awakened by her mother requesting her to read the back of a tampon box because Jeanie was not acting like herself. She had complained of a headache shortly before she began slurring her speech and became very confused. Jeanie, like many teenage girls, preferred tampons, and her mother worried that she had toxic shock syndrome. We are unaware of how much time passed, but her stepfather carried Jeanie out to the vehicle. She lay across Heather's lap while their mother drove to the nearest hospital. Heather continued to talk to Jeanie about Albert, Rob, me, and our dogs, hoping to keep her alert, but she was unresponsive upon arrival.

Three days prior, as Albert and I were saying our goodnights to the kids and giving hugs, Albert noticed one of Jeanie's pupils had rapidly enlarged and immediately returned to normal. It happened so suddenly that by the time he had me look, it was normal. We had planned to inform her physician when we returned for the follow-up because Jeanie did not have any complaints.

Albert and I left immediately for the hospital. Upon our arrival, a medical helicopter was running and waiting near the ER entrance. As we rushed by it, Albert said, "It better not be here for Jeanie." We walked through the automatic glass doors and immediately the girls' mother screamed at me. "You killed her. You gave her toxic shock syndrome." I was stunned to say the least, but the emergency physician was standing next to her. He said, "That is not correct. You need to get to Bronson Methodist Hospital because she is being airlifted right now."

We arrived in Kalamazoo only to have to wait for what seemed like forever. Time stood still. And then we were allowed into the intensive care unit, led by a medical physician. Our daughter was lying in a hospital gown, on life support, and her head had been shaved for a stent that was placed into her brain. The doctors were checking for brain activity. For the next forty-eight hours, our family was numb. We were helpless. As I sat for hours on end next to Jeanie, holding her hand, I prayed to God. I asked Him to take her if she was never going to recover or be the same. It was shocking to see her lifeless body lying there.

A little after midnight, a male physician entered Jeanie's room and began looking over her body. He felt the temperature on her extremities and stood in front of the machines and turned to me and asked how I was doing. I responded, "Today is the day. If she is going to die, today is the day." You see, Jeanie would frequently come up and grab my hand and say, as she pointed to the diamonds in my ring, "past, present, future." And then she would go about her business. "Today is our third anniversary." I didn't expect him to understand, and he recited the words "Happy Anniversary," but they dissolved into thin air.

By 6:00 p.m., Jeanie was declared brain dead. Our family was beyond devastated. We were utterly broken. Select family were directed to a consultation room. The physician confirmed that a blood clot ruptured in Jeanie's brain stem. It was a complication of an unknown birth defect. She suffered a massive intracranial hemorrhage, a ruptured arteriovenous malformation. He then asked what the wishes of our family were. I spoke up and mentioned that our family recently had a conversation about death, dying, and organ donation. Jeanie chose cremation and organ donation. Her mother bellowed out, "You are not burning her like trash." Albert and Jeanie's mother met with another individual. It was decided that, in fact, Jeanie would be an organ donor. Jeanie's generosity saved and benefited many lives. She gave life to four very sick people.

The following few days were a blur. The school was notified. An appointment was made for us to come collect Jeanie's things. Upon arrival, we sat in the office while her belongings were presented to us. Jeanie had strategically punctured a pair of earrings through the material on her binder that my son gifted her with several years earlier. And on another folder, her name was written with a heart above the "I" in her name as I had always written it. It was a special visual. And I truly believe these items were special messages to us, just as her death was on our anniversary. Jeanie proclaimed thirteen was her lucky number. She passed away on the thirteenth, at the age of thirteen.

Albert and I received notification that a local church wanted to assist our family. Everything would be taken care of even though our family did not attend a church; we gratefully accepted. The church was a welcome help and source of strength as we grieved. Jeanie's memorial was held at Douglas Community Church. Although many friends, students, and families were in attendance, my mother and sister were not present. My mother never accepted Jeanie. She did not understand how I could love a stepchild as my own. And Amy had no desire to be there because her alcohol was more important. Neither one cared about anyone besides their own needs. As much as it deeply hurt that they were not there for me, I did have my dad and a couple of half-siblings there.

My son and Jeanie had a special connection. Rob was broken but wanted to share his heart with those in attendance. He pulled out a notebook where he had written down his thoughts about Jeanie after she had died, and he began to share his deepest thoughts. My son thanked God for being with Jeanie because we were told it was a miracle she lived that long. This was the first time my son publicly acknowledged God. He was unashamed. Rob, at age fifteen, said, "For Jeanie, I'm going to try and live my dream for her because she gives me that motive that gets me going. She was part of my life; half my heart ran because of her." I don't have the words to explain the beauty and sadness of that day. On one hand, the blessings of complete strangers giving of their time and resources to assist our family in our greatest time of need and my son speaking about God in front of his classmates, friends, and extended family, were so deeply touching to me, because as his mother, that is all I wanted to teach him, the love of our heavenly Father and for my son to truly know that He is *always* with him. That day I heard my teenage son speak out about God. I am forever blessed. And on the other hand, there was the grim reality that our family was never going to be the same. Our "three stooges" were now two. Days later, on my husband's birthday, we buried Jeanie's cremains in the church's garden.

Since receiving the unexpected phone call notifying Albert that Jeanie was in the hospital, our family had been nonstop on the go. After a few weeks, everything had come to a halt. Our family did not seek outside counseling to deal with our grief; we chose to help each other as best we were able. One evening, while my husband and I were alone, he literally dropped to his knees while looking at a picture of Jeanie. Albert began weeping. I wrapped my arms around him, but he was inconsolable. At that heart-wrenching moment, the only thing I knew to do was to grab my Bible. I was emotionally bankrupt and desperate for God to help my husband. I knew God was right there with us, but I needed Him to console my husband. I paged through God's Word and recited whatever Scripture was illuminated to me to help comfort my husband, and it worked.

We all grieve in different ways. Although Albert didn't show it, he carried anger deep within. Rob shared his feelings with us often. Heather did not talk much. She informed us that at her mother's home, they were not allowed to talk about Jeanie, and all pictures of her were taken down. This was extremely difficult for us to hear, because we did exactly the opposite. At our home, we talked about Jeanie and laughed and cried at various times too. Our family held each other up. It was the grace and mercy of God. When one of us was in need, another was strong. Many days and nights we intentionally sat together and shared stories of Jeanie, but the common thing that brought us joy was remembering her infectious laugh. And knowing today that we will be reunited brings us great comfort.

Our family did the best we could to persevere one day at a time.

Posthumous Diploma

During the year when Jeanie was to graduate, my son contacted the Saugatuck High School and requested that his sister be remembered during her graduating class ceremony. Rob arranged for the memorial, including the posthumous diploma. Shortly afterward, I was contacted by a staff member and asked to speak at the graduation ceremony. We invited Jeanie's mother to attend to show her love during this time and asked her to sit with us. She did. The day had arrived. Albert and I were directed to our seats. My son, knowing this would be an emotional day, chose to sit in the bleachers with his girlfriend and his father.

One by one the graduates entered the gymnasium. The females were carrying a single orange flower as they went to their seats. They had an empty seat on the end with a single orange flower placed on it in remembrance of Jeanie.

My stomach felt a bit nervous because there were hundreds of people in attendance. I had never spoken in public before such a large crowd, but God was using me and stretching me in new ways all the time. The principal said, "Please welcome Tracy Michaud, presenting the first Jeanie Michaud Memorial Scholarship." The audience clapped. He handed me the microphone, and although I had memorized what I had planned to say in honor of our daughter, I read from my note card. I looked up a time or two but held back my tears. Albert wept the entire time I spoke. Both he and Heather clutched their tear-soaked tissues as I continued and announced that the first scholarship was being presented to Jeanie's best friend, Amanda. I was told later by a friend in attendance that there wasn't a dry eye in sight. The diplomas were handed out, and there was one left sitting on the table; the announcer said, "Jeanie Michaud." The principal stepped down from the stage as the graduates stood and turned toward our family, the entire audience stood too. The principal greeted me with a hug and presented the posthumous diploma to Albert. Our hearts were overwhelmed with emotion. I thanked my son for initiating this for our daughter. God used Rob to impact our family. It was a powerful and healing day. The tragedy and pain we endured was turned into joy as our family blessed others. And although we only continued with the scholarship for three more years, we had great joy knowing we were able to financially assist a few graduates toward their future.

Seven years after Jeanie died, our family, by the grace of God, relocated her cremains and reburied them in a cemetery near our home. We had a customized headstone made with Jeanie's very own handwriting etched into it. God had fulfilled His promise to our family. He says in His Word, "Weeping may endure for a night, but joy comes in the morning" (Psalm 30:5 NKJV).

My Mother's Story

Three months prior to Jeanie's death, my mother was having trouble breathing and asked me to go with her to the emergency room at Blodgett Hospital in Grand Rapids. I got out of the car and told the security officer that my mother needed help. She could not breathe. They quickly escorted her in by a wheelchair. Many tests were performed. My mother was diagnosed with terminal lung cancer. She was already in stage four and had a large tumor growing in her right lung. As unpleasant as our relationship was, I told my mother that I would stay with her in the hospital until she was discharged. I loved my mother and desired to be near her during this horrific and lonely time in her life. My family did not quite understand why I would stay with her, but they fully accepted my sacrifice.

For the next twenty-one days, I remained by my mother's side. I kept in contact with my family by using my mother's cell phone. Chemotherapy began immediately, and we were told she had approximately six months to live. I read the Bible to my mother while she lay in the hospital bed crying. She repeatedly asked me what I wanted from her. I responded, "Nothing. I love you." My mother couldn't fathom the idea that I would remain by her side, because she had failed to do that for me. She was suspicious of my intentions and told me that I owed her eighteen months of her life that she had spent going back and forth to the hospital, to lawyer appointments, and so forth. Oh my goodness, it was not easy. My sister became overly jealous and stayed with us for a few nights too. My mother and sister reminded me that I was not listed in the will and I was not receiving anything. As much as that hurt to hear them say that, I truly didn't want any material item. I just wanted my mother to love me, to accept me, and to talk to me.

Upon my mother's discharge from the hospital, Amy and I took turns staying with our mother. We alternated three days on, four days off, with our mother's third husband coming to help too.

My sister was a severe alcoholic, a mean drunk who did not care for our mother as well as she thought she did. Many nights I received phone calls from my mother crying because Amy was not helping her. My mother and I talked a lot on the phone. I enjoyed these talks, but they were nothing of real importance, more so to pass the time until she was ready to go to bed.

For two months, I helped my mother. She was physically independent and seemed to be doing fine, but I helped her anyway. While at my mother's home, she did not want my family over. She would not allow me to use her computer, watch television, or even use her phone. We just sat at the kitchen table. Many times we sat in silence, or she would be on the phone talking, and I would just have to hear a one-sided conversation. She isolated me away from my family. It was awful.

I pondered how to tell my mother that I wanted to go home. My husband and kids were attending a karaoke party, and I wanted to spend time with them. That day, I decided I just couldn't do it anymore. I mentioned to her that I would like to go and hang out with my family. Albert and I didn't have cell phones at the time, so I could not get ahold of him. My mother jumped up and said, "I'll take you. Let's go!" I was so relieved. I didn't want to be at her house any longer. She did not need me on a day-to-day basis. We left almost immediately. As my mother drove down the highway, she kept saying, "I should just run us off the road. I'm gonna die anyway." I was filled with fear knowing she truly didn't care about herself at that point. I didn't respond. We arrived in Grand Junction. I had mixed emotions. I was happy to be able to spend time with my family but saddened that my mother expected me to be at her beck and call when she was still independent. It was a taxing situation. As I was getting out of the car, very angrily my mother said, "You screwed [a polite interpretation of her wording] me over. I don't want your help anymore." Then she drove away. I focused my attention on my family. We took some pictures. I am forever grateful that we did, because it's the last one I have of Jeanie and me.

A year passed before my mother actually spoke to me. When she felt her death was upon her, she had Amy dial the phone to call me. Days later, my mother was airlifted to Grand Rapids and placed in the intensive critical care unit. When I got to the hospital, she was on life support. Amy stood in the corner with both of her arms wrapped around a folder which contained our mother's will.

I leaned into my mother and told her that I was there. She opened her eyes and began mouthing words to me. To everyone's surprise, I was fully able to recite word for word what she was saying. Even the nursing staff was amazed. It was a gift I believe God gave to me. Anyone who wanted to communicate with my mother would ask me to interpret. After a short stay, she was discharged. She had regurgitated food into her lungs. It was not cancer-related. I believe this brief hospitalization was an eye-opening reality to my mother's life situation, that in fact she was facing death. I noticed my mother began to change a bit, to soften. I wasn't sure what was going on, but I believed God was working on her. Maybe the Scriptures I had read to her from the Bible had penetrated after all. The next three months was evidence of God working on my mother's heart. She wanted to make things right, to put her affairs in order, and try to heal our relationship.

One mid-September day, my mother called and asked Albert and me to come over. Although he was hesitant, we went. Once we arrived, my mother told my husband something was wrong with her car and asked him to look it over. While he was outside, my mother told me she had a dream the night before. She told me that God had spoken to her. She said, "He told me to buy you a new car." I cried. I knew it must be God, since she was a lover of money and had never acknowledged God previously.

Albert walked into the house and saw me bawling. I immediately told him what she said. Albert responded by telling her what needed to be replaced on her car. She requested that he fix it so she could get around. He did so for the love of keeping the peace. Three weeks later, I picked up my brand-new bright red Monte Carlo from Robert DeNooyer Chevrolet in Holland. It was a beautiful sight. I was grateful to God and my mother.

On Christmas Eve, my mother invited my son and me over to her home. We drove separately. At this time, Amy and her boyfriend, who I will call Sam, lived in the fully finished basement, but they were not home. My mother had some belongings that she wanted to give to us. She asked us to look around the house and see if there was anything that either of us would like to take before she died. Rob accepted only what she offered him. I told her that I had happy memories of listening to her records with her when I was a little girl. She gave me her entire collection. My son left shortly afterward so my mother and I could visit.

I brought along a song I had recorded for my mother called "Hurt," sung by Christina Aguilera. I printed the lyrics in very large print so she would be able to read along. I asked her if I could play a song for her. She agreed. We went into her computer room. She placed the disc into the computer. The song played, and she read the words on the page. My mother began crying. She sobbed and sobbed.

I was standing behind her on my crutches while she sat in her chair directly in front of the computer. I wrapped my arms around her, and tears started flowing down my cheeks. My mother had blamed me for everything that went wrong in her life. The song apologizes for blaming someone else because they are "hurt." If you are unfamiliar with the song, I encourage you to listen to it. It was so powerful and moving that my mother apologized to me for my childhood. She told me how proud she was of me for moving along in life with one leg and not letting it bother me. And then she asked to have the song played at her funeral and told me I needed to gather some pictures of myself and my son to bring to the funeral home to include, as well as inform them to add my family to her obituary. I was deeply hurt that she had planned not to acknowledge me at her funeral, but we had begun an honest mother-daughter relationship. It only lasted for two months, but I was grateful to have that time with my mother.

The Deuces

It was 6:00 a.m. on February 22, 2007, when my mother woke up screaming my name. For the past several days, I had been staying with her, at her request. At this point, hospice was involved. A hospital bed was placed in the center of her living room. My mother was bedridden and had been catheterized. Startled awake, I sat up to see what she needed and suddenly slipped down and completely off the recliner. It took me a few seconds to get up off the floor and sit back into the chair. As I repositioned myself, my sister came running upstairs because she heard the commotion. Our mother then said, "I'm so happy!" Amy asked her why. She replied, "Because I'm not dead!" Amy did not respond; it was too early for her to be up after drinking the evening before. She left the room.

Five days earlier, I was certain it would be the last day with my mother on earth. I moved the chair I was sitting in toward her and made direct eye contact and told my mother I loved her. She replied, "I love you too, Tracy." And then she grabbed the side of my head and pulled me toward her and kissed me three times, real fast on my lips.

She said again, "I love you." I then hugged her, and she said, "Don't wait too long before you come to see me in heaven." I replied, "I won't." We said our goodbyes with love.

That morning my mother was more alert than she had been for days. I got up, opened the blinds, and sat near the edge of the bed to be closer to her. She turned her head and looked at me and asked, "Am I going to die today"? I replied, "Mom, I don't know. Only God knows." I asked my mother if she felt she was going to heaven, if she'd talked to God about her life. She said, "Yes. I was ready many times for God to just take me. I don't understand." I was only able to say, "It wasn't your time."

I offered her some water. She sucked many ounces down very quickly and said, "I should have listened to everybody." She was thirsty. She hadn't eaten anything in days aside from sips of Carnation Instant Breakfast here and there. I asked her if she wanted her favorite pop, Coca Cola Classic. She said, "Yes," and Amy brought her a can. She took a sip, then wanted a new one. She was weak and unsteady but insisted on drinking the second one by herself using a straw. She then wanted to get out of bed. Amy and I both witnessed her sit up and yell, "Do you know what it's like to be in bed for three days?!" In unison, we responded, "Yes." She plopped back down on the bed, and Amy applied her pain medication.

As the hours passed by, slowly my mother deteriorated. Amy contacted our great aunt. She came over and took my sister to Subway. They left me alone with my mother in her death-rattle state. I called Albert from the bathroom, crying, and asked him to come because I needed him.

My sister and great aunt returned and were in the living room with my mother when my husband arrived just before 6:00 p.m. As he walked into the house, I wrapped my arms around him and sobbed. Albert and I were in the kitchen. He was able to hear the sounds that my mother made, the gasping, gurgling noise that made me feel so helpless. My mind wondered, *When, Lord? When are you going to take her?* I pleaded out loud, while crying to Albert, saying, "God, please take my mom peacefully!" She was so loud. I just cried, "Please, God, take my mom peacefully."

Seconds later, our great aunt came into the kitchen. "Tracy, you better come now." Albert and I immediately followed her into the living room. Amy was sitting on the bed holding my mom's left hand. I sat on the bed holding my mom's right hand. I leaned in and told her, "It's okay. I love you, Mom." At 6:35 p.m., she took three more breaths—they were *completely silent*. My pleas were answered. Her eyes were closed. I looked at her face for what seemed like forever. I felt relieved. She was free from a life of pain, and we had forgiven each other. The past is the past. We made up for each of our mistakes. I felt at peace. It was over. I kissed my mom on the forehead, and I went to the bathroom so I didn't have to watch them take her out the front door on a stretcher. I broke down in the bathroom with my husband by my side. I was so hurt. The mother I had always wanted was gone, but she was able to have both of her daughters by her side as she passed. Our great aunt then requested that I write and present the eulogy. All things happen for a reason. Only God knows why.

In Memory of My Mother

God was not only my strength at this time; He was carrying me. I knew for my mother, I couldn't let others know exactly what she had been through, and truth be told, nobody else wanted to know. As I shared the tragedy of my sister's and my separate accidents, I did bend the truth in saying our mother was supportive of both of us, when in fact she had only been supportive of Amy, but I had forgiven her. Others had always judged her, but they didn't know her background. My mother was a deeply wounded woman who vowed to take care of herself because her parents had failed. My mother was a lover of self and money. She was a gambler, and all who knew her knew this about her. She did not have Jesus in her life until the end, but my sister and I celebrate knowing we will reunite in heaven. My heart was with my mom, not with the body that lay in that casket. For the love of my mother, I spoke and recounted her life.

One week after our mother's funeral, Amy called to let me know she was going to give me some of the money that remained in our mother's checking account. I thanked her and told her that with the money, I planned to return to college. Three months later, I was a full-time student. My dream had once again become a reality. I had hoped to finish college, to help others, and be a role model for my children. To teach them to never give up despite obstacles, but once again, life circumstances changed my plans.

CHAPTER 10

Blessings Abound

For we walk by faith, not by sight.
2 Corinthians 5:7 (NKJV)

WINTER HAD ARRIVED. THINGS SEEMED TO BE GOING WELL IN MY life. I was enjoying this part of my journey. With the money I received from my mom, I enrolled in the bachelor's degree in human services program. My goal was to become a social worker and help others in their everyday lives. I was getting As in my classes. I was so proud of myself. But mostly, I hoped to be a positive role model for my children.

I began experiencing severe pain in my left elbow. Pushing the wheelchair through the snow-covered parking lot at the university was not worth the frustration, and the entrance to the University of Phoenix at the West Michigan campus was not handicap accessible. For the time being, I had to switch my schedule to online classes but decided to represent disabled individuals by requesting that an automatic door be installed. I contacted the school office with my request for changes to be made on campus. I had to make the request in writing, then it was sent to the campus ADA compliance officer in Phoenix, Arizona. I had to go through a step-by-step process of self-disclosure of my disability, including documentation proving that it was at least three years prior to attending classes. I received an email back from the disability services advisor. He informed me the requests I had made were going to be implemented. We communicated by email until the accommodations were in place. Through my disability and physical pain, I was able to make a difference for many others. I felt empowered. I felt valuable.

Early spring I returned to the University of Phoenix campus. I felt peaceful and excited to be back. As I pulled into the handicap parking spot nearest the entrance of the building, I noticed several individuals using the automatic doors as they entered the building. They had their hands full, so the automatic doors were also a blessing for them. It felt good to be used by God in helping others, because that's all I desire to do. It was truly a joy-filled moment.

Part of my degree included an outside internship. There were several places to choose from, but my heart was set on American Red Cross. The truth is, I specifically wanted to intern there because of the gratitude I had to all the blood donors who gave selflessly, saving my life so long ago. While interning at the American Red Cross, I answered an incoming call. It was my physician's office. Earlier that morning, I went to the laboratory to have blood drawn because I had been chronically fatigued for over two years. This call was requesting that I return to the laboratory and have blood drawn again to confirm elevated liver enzymes.

The following day I was in my home office working on a paper for one of my college classes, and Albert was out in the living room. The phone rang so I quickly answered. My physician was on the other end. I heard him say, "You have something that you have had for some time now. Tracy, I want you to do some research on hepatitis C, and I will call you back soon." Tears began to stream down my face as I knew my life was about to change. Things had finally been looking up, but now, once again, things were uncertain.

As I turned around, my husband was standing in the doorway. He noticed the emotion, the look of helplessness and uncertainty. With tears dripping down my face, I immediately told him what the doctor said. Albert calmly and confidently replied, "Tracy, we will get through this."

I had a peaceful feeling inside, but truly I was numb. I knew God had a reason for allowing everything. However, I did not understand why another life-altering diagnosis would be allowed to enter my life. I wondered, *Why can't I once and for all put the past tragedy behind me and flourish in life with my husband and children? Why can't I reach my dreams of college graduation and career goals?* I asked God, "How will I continue to help others if I am sick and I die?" Nothing made sense to me then.

Albert and I met with a liver specialist. We were informed there was no cure for hepatitis C. However, treatment was available. He explained my genotype, 1a, saying it was the hardest to treat and would require close to a full year of medications and careful monitoring. Apparently, I acquired the virus as a direct result of high-volume blood and blood products received in 1987—the blood transfusions from my accident. I was able to accept this information because I had learned much during my internship at the American Red Cross. It was not a coincidence that I was there. God knew I would face this trial and prepared me in advance. His ways are not ours, and it is never for us to try to figure out. We are to fully place our trust in Him and know that He makes all things new.

I chose not to undergo treatment. I know it sounds risky, but I was placing my life in God's hands. Although Albert supported my decision, he really wanted me to get treated, even though there was no cure. I continually prayed for guidance. I switched my college classes to online courses and later withdrew. College was no longer a priority. I was fighting for my life.

For the next *six* years, I attended various medical appointments, which included a liver biopsy. I was given a script to obtain medical marijuana for pain because everything we put in our mouths is filtered by our liver, and for someone who has an impaired liver, decreasing and avoiding additional toxins is vital. I was approved by the State of Michigan. I located a caregiver and purchased a vaporizer to administer the marijuana, smoke-free. I learned more about marijuana; not only did it assist with pain but it also reduced inflammation. I must admit, the relief I attained was almost instantaneous. But the stigma associated with it overwhelmed me. Like the Bible says in John 10:10,

"The thief comes only in order to steal and kill and destroy. I came that they may have and enjoy life, and have it in abundance [to the full, till it overflows]" (AMP). Although I was receiving pain relief through an alternative measure, it became an internal struggle. I believed the lie that somehow what I was doing was wrong. The devil is the liar! Today in Michigan, for adults over the age of twenty-one, marijuana is legal. I'm so grateful it is accessible to those who need it, even if it's frowned upon by those who disagree or do not understand. I would *never* expect someone to understand the physical chronic pain I have, nor would I want anyone to have to endure the tragedy I have to fully understand.

As the days and weeks went by, I often found myself thinking about my life and what was in store for my future. I didn't want to die. I just wanted to be happy. I shed so many tears. I cried out to God like a little child begging Him to save me. I asked Him to guide every decision and to show me what to do because I was helpless. I wondered if God would physically save me once again from death because of the poor choices I had made as a broken girl. Was He that forgiving? I fully surrendered to God. I repented again for my sins that I had committed during my entire life without Him.

After a routine lab draw, I received a letter from my physician stating my liver enzymes were elevated. He requested I call the office but I didn't. I was numb after reading it. I prayed. It was then when I felt a nudge to call Mayo Clinic in Rochester, Minnesota, and request a second opinion. So I did. I was scheduled exactly five weeks later, for an appointment on Monday, June 13. This was confirmation and God's favor because the scheduler told me most appointments were at least ninety days out. I felt hopeful. I recalled a verse in James, asking, "Is anyone among you sick? Let them call the elders of the church to pray over them and anoint them with oil in the name of the Lord" (5:14). A week before my appointment, our pastor, an elder, and a few friends prayed over me. Our pastor asked, "Specifically what is it that you want?" I replied, "When I get to Mayo Clinic, I want the doctor to ask, 'Why are you here?'" In my heart I believed the results would show I was healed and there was nothing wrong with me.

The day had arrived. I, along with my friend, who graciously and selflessly joined me on the eleven-hour trip, met the medical professional. Upon him entering the examination room, with my medical binder under his arm, he sat down and asked, "Why are you here?" I was floored. That was definitely a God-wink with Renee as a witness.

The hepatologist said in his report, despite how long I'd had this virus, there was "essentially no chance of liver disease"; my liver had no damage, and he didn't see any further complications. My liver felt normal during the exam, and the MRI showed mild hepatic fibrosis, which was nothing to be concerned over. He recommended waiting a few more years to treat anything because new meds would be available to possibly eradicate the virus.

I am amazed how God loves me so much that He put in my heart to get a second opinion. And that He would care enough to answer my prayer so directly as evidenced by the words of the doctor at Mayo! Sometimes when we don't have that inner peace and we need to make a tough decision, it's God's nudging to seek a different way. In my case, this was definitely true. *Thank you, Lord.* Although I did not hear that I was healed, I fully trusted God was working on my behalf. I knew I was not alone in my fight.

Healing Balm of Gilead

Another four years passed. It was time. The FDA approved a once-a-day tablet for individuals living with hepatitis C, genotype 1a. I completed a checklist of pretesting and pretreatment procedures, which included a CT scan of my liver, and was given a series of vaccines.

Albert took off work to attend the very first day of treatment. I was comforted by him being with me to hear firsthand what was expected, what side effects to watch for, and to assist me throughout this long-awaited regimen. Having been informed of the risks and benefits, I elected to continue. I was given a summary sheet with all the important dates listed and an emergency contact with my team nurse. It was stressed over and over again the importance of taking the medication *exactly* as prescribed and to stay hydrated. For the next fifty-six days, I had to abide by a strict schedule. I was warned to take my proton pump inhibitor (stomach pill) at the same time as Harvoni. Even one slipup and the treatment could fail.

For the most part, the treatment went well. However, one particular day I was so exhausted and cried uncontrollably. My husband was so kind and compassionate throughout. He escorted me to bed and covered me up, suggesting I physically rest. Albert gently reminded me that my body was ingesting a powerful drug and that this too shall pass. He was correct. The next morning, I declared, "This is the day the LORD has made; *I will* rejoice and be glad in it!" (Psalm 118:24 NKJV, author's paraphrase).

I fasted and completed my blood work for week four, week eight, and the final lab draw three months later. Before each blood draw, I prayed and declared, "Lord, I know you are my healer! I pray in Jesus' name and by your stripes, heal me. *Be healed* with your blood transfusion. Hepatitis C, be gone! Healed completely. *No virus!* I am claiming healing, healing in my mind and liver. Free completely."

If the lab draw revealed "undetected," that would mean I had a sustained virologic response (SVR) and I would be considered cured. Each result came back the same: *undetected!* Twenty-eight years after acquiring the virus, I was cured. *I am cured.* I was overjoyed. *I am overjoyed.* I was grateful. *I am still grateful.* God truly gave me His blood transfusion. I am cleansed and pure, and He alone gets the glory. Praise God for Gilead Sciences. *Thank you, Jesus.* "And He said to her, 'Daughter, your faith has made you well. Go in peace, and be healed of your affliction'" (Mark 5:34 NKJV).

More Gifts from Above

More blessings were on the horizon for me. It was a brisk January day, and the sun had blessed us throughout. Albert and I had many unknown situations on our plate, and the beauty of the sun setting always brings me peace, so we decided to go watch the sunset on Lake

Michigan. Whenever I feel an urgent need or have to make an important decision, I get in my vehicle and drive four miles to Lake Michigan
and pray. I know that God is with me no matter where I am, but the
expanse of the lake and the breeze cover me with His peace every time.
Many days and evenings, throughout the year, I go to the lake just to
gaze at the surrounding beauty and thank God for who He is and all
He has done in my life.

Days later, Albert and I attended a scheduled meeting with a
team of professionals from many companies. After months of negoti-
ating details in the home evaluation situation, all parties had agreed
to renovate my manufactured home, making it handicap accessible.
I was beyond grateful. But not long after the meeting, I received a
phone call from the lawyer representing me. He told me the reno-
vation project was too expensive but said there was another option.
He told me the insurance company was willing to pay off my current
mortgage, in which I immediately asked him to repeat himself. He
did. I began bawling. He said, "The most cost-effective option is to
demolish the existing dwelling and rebuild." He continued saying that
a case manager would assist in the moving process and *all expenses
would be paid in full.* He informed me that I would be fully involved
and I would be required to be on-site at times to do custom measure-
ments throughout the building process.

A custom, barrier-free home was going to be built for me. The
lawyer reassured me that he would assist throughout the process, pro
bono. My mother's auto insurance had lifetime medical benefits, but
she failed to follow through with getting the assistance decades earlier.
His desire was to assist me in obtaining the proper medical equipment
necessary to remain independent. Although my tears of gratitude were
heard through the phone, words cannot describe how I felt at that
exact moment. I knew God was at the center of it all. He was orches-
trating every detail of my life, and I was in awe. How could I not be?
It was all Him! Only He knew my deepest desires and all the things
I needed; only He knew the deep, dark thoughts in my mind, the
struggles I had of not feeling worthy. One thing I knew for sure is

when God chooses to bless, He doesn't mess around. He goes above and beyond our wildest dreams.

Our temporary home was a beautiful arrangement at a well-known hotel, which allowed our two little dogs to be with us. We moved into a two-bedroom, two-bath suite, with a living room and little kitchen. My greatest joy was the access to the indoor pool and breakfast and dinner buffets. Albert was hired into a company near our home a few months earlier, and by now, Rob was a senior in high school. He was fully involved in sports, worked part time, and was applying to colleges. At that time, I attended classes myself. Heather was a junior in high school and worked most weekends; she came to visit as her schedule permitted. Life was busy, but we knew this living situation was temporary. Albert and I received the keys to move into our new home on the one-year anniversary of my mother's passing. It was truly a blessing from God. I had complete peace.

I continued to receive one amazing gift after another to assist with my activities of daily living. A roll-in shower chair was delivered for safe and independent shower access. I was measured for a custom power chair to help eliminate strain on my overly exerted shoulders and elbows in an effort to avoid future surgery. I have had this power chair for ten years, and I do not see surgery in my future. Praise the Lord! Although initially I was hesitant to accept the power chair, it has become one of the biggest aids in helping me move about my home while doing chores. I am so thankful for it. I cannot imagine my life without it. I still regularly use a manual wheelchair outside of my home, but when pain or weather are a factor, I use the power chair.

I was also given an electric scooter to independently enjoy our property. This too has been a life-changing mobility aid. I am able to enjoy the great outdoors without assistance. It is such a wonderful gift to be alone in the woods with my Creator. He is so faithful. After the power chair was ordered, I was told I would be receiving a brand-new side-entry, wheelchair-accessible van, complete with hand controls. I would not have to endure one more day of struggling to lift my manual wheelchair in and out of the car. I would not have to worry about my safety one more Michigan winter either; I could just roll up the ramp and into my van. I was blessed beyond measure and forever grateful.

But God wasn't done yet. As long as I can remember, possibly before my son was born, I began speaking out loud that one day I would have an indoor pool. I truly never could have imagined that my husband, by the grace of God, would bless me with that dream. Albert had watched me, through all four seasons, go to the aquatic center and local pools for therapy. One particular winter morning, while my husband was at work, I went to the nearest pool. I grabbed my duffle bag from the back seat, which contained my drinking water, aquatic shoe, bathing suit, and towel. I exited my van with my keys in hand. I closed the van door and turned my wheelchair around to head inside. And I was stuck! It was negative temperatures outside, and I did not have my cell phone on me. I had accidently left it in the van. I struggled to move, but my wheelchair would not budge. Thankfully, an employee who recognized me noticed I was struggling. She came out to the parking lot to assist me inside. I appreciated her help because at this point my fingers were frozen and I was beginning to panic. After I shared this incident with my husband, he was on a mission. For weeks on end, after he came home from work and on the weekends, Albert went outside to our attached garage and began to prepare it for a swim spa. For over five years, I have not had to leave my home for aquatic exercise. It has been one of the greatest blessings in my life. I am forever grateful to my husband, who loves me unconditionally, gives of himself to help me in many ways, and *never* complains in doing so. Albert is truly a gift from God. He may be a quiet man, but he is wise and has a servant's heart. To God be all the glory.

God had given me so much more than I could have ever asked for or imagined. The blessings just kept coming, overwhelming me with His grace, mercy, and love. Physical healing, material blessings to make my life easier, and charity I would never be able to pay back. Truly, God's graciousness knows no bounds. But even with all these material blessings in my life, I continued to struggle internally. Without my approval, unworthiness moved into my home and roomed with guilt. They became well-acquainted friends—friends I no longer wanted lingering in my life but didn't know how to get rid of. This was next on God's agenda for me.

CHAPTER 11

Faith, Forgiveness, and Healing

So do not throw away your confidence; it will be richly rewarded.
You need to persevere so that when you have done the will of God, you will receive
what he has promised.

Hebrews 10:35–36

EVER SINCE MY SON WAS A LITTLE BOY, I SPOKE TO HIM ABOUT GOD. I reminded Rob that God was always with him and repeatedly told him that everything happened for a reason. Only God knew why. Trust Him and talk to Him and He will help you. Little did I know that *my son* would lead me into the arms of Jesus.

It was Christmas break, and Rob was home from his sophomore year in college at Ferris State University in Big Rapids, Michigan, about two hours from our home. Rob came home to spend time with our family. Two weeks prior, he had surprised me on my birthday with reservations at a restaurant for the two of us to spend some quality time together. Rob and I have always had a close relationship. I am grateful for our bond. My cup overflows with the love and respect my son showers upon me; he is a true blessing from God above. I treasure our time together.

Rob confided in me that he wanted to join the air force. This was devastating news to me. I had already lost one child, and at that time my health was not so great. The only thing that came out of my mouth when we discussed it was that I loved him and I supported his decision. I noticed the relief in his eyes, since he knew how important a college education was to me. My son left college and moved back home, enlisted in the air force, and began training.

After Rob moved back home, he approached me and asked, "Mother, would you like to go to church with me?" Instantaneously I replied no. It was because I was afraid of judgment from others that I had said it so quickly. My son relentlessly asked me for the next two weeks, and each time I said no. Rob even mentioned we could "church hop" until we found one I liked. However, each time I told him no. And then God spoke to me clearly, asking, "Tracy, you would do *anything* for your children, wouldn't you?" I knew exactly at that moment that I was to go with my nineteen-year-old son to church. So the following weekend when he asked, we went. Later in the day, I asked Rob, "What made you ask me to go to church?" He replied, "God." No explanations, just "God." The truth is, God knew my heart and the *only* person in the world I would have gone to church for is my son. My first experience entering the church was a warm welcome and guidance to the sanctuary because we had entered through the wrong doors. It was a friendly and caring environment, and there were people of all ages. I felt welcomed.

Only two Sundays passed by, and my husband noticed a drastic change in me. Albert said, "Tracy, something is different about you." I told him that if he wanted what I had, he should come with us to church, and the following week he began attending too.

Six months after we began attending church, Albert and I, along with my son, publicly professed our faith in Jesus, and afterward we were baptized in Lake Michigan. We were washed clean by the blood of our Savior. Several family members and friends were present to witness the dedication of our lives surrendered to our Savior. That was a significant day in my life and in the lives of my husband and son. The Bible tells us in 2 Corinthians 5:17, "Therefore, if anyone is in Christ, he is a new creation; old things have passed away; behold, all things have become new" (NKJV). Our old life was gone; the new had arrived.

As a born-again Christian, I was on a new mission of placing my trust in God, fully relying on Him to fix me. It felt great knowing

God had forgiven me, but I still had a lot of work to do to forgive myself. I was ready to tackle something that I knew had to be done, which was getting off all prescription medications. I enlisted the help of my husband and a nurse practitioner, who is also a close friend. I requested they take note of my mental and emotional state, because against medical advice, I was taking myself off of them.

You see, years earlier, when I was originally sent to talk to a counselor, I was a desperate mess. I was in need of emotional healing and relief from shame and guilt. The doctor diagnosed me as having a mood disorder, so he prescribed medications that would uplift my mood and make me happy. But no medicine does that. I ingested the medication as prescribed for over five years and did not feel any different. In spite of the warnings against stopping abruptly, I did. I just expected God to take care of me. He was faithful. I did not have any side effects of stopping the mood-stabilizing meds.

Being off of these medications actually made me feel better knowing that I wasn't ingesting all the man-made chemicals any longer. But what made a tremendous difference in my daily life was reading the Bible, God's Word—getting the truth in me and repenting of my sins, the deep soul work we all must do at one point in our lives. Jesus and His Word were what really transformed my life. What I needed the whole time was the truth about His unconditional love and forgiveness; His comforting words that I belong, I matter, and I am forgiven. There was no reason to carry the heavy weight of shame and guilt any longer. The truth of Christ set me free.

Today I am blessed to say that I wouldn't have changed a thing I have gone through because it brought me to where I am today. I am not saying that everyone taking meds should toss them out like I did, but I am suggesting that you get into the Bible and dig deep for the answers you so desperately long for. They are in there. All of them. Romans 12:2 tells us, "Do not conform to the pattern of this world, but be transformed by the renewing of your mind. Then you will be able to test and approve what God's will is—his good, pleasing and perfect will." God's Word transformed my life and renewed my mind.

I am not perfect in any way, but I am His daughter, and He has always loved me and knew that one day I would share with the world what He, and He alone, has accomplished in and through my life. He is faithful and will bind your wounds too. Open your heart, your mind, and your Bible, and ask Him to change you. He will. I have to be honest and say there were times that I didn't even recognize who I was becoming. And looking back, too, I am amazed at the "old me," because although I lived in her body, I don't recognize her as "me." She is like an old friend I knew intimately so very long ago. All I can say is, "Thank you, Jesus, for never giving up on me and for saving me."

Although I am genuinely happy and content, my physical body continues to have issues as you would expect when you've had the kind of injuries I have. Once I became a professing Christian, I was told that marijuana, medical or not, was frowned upon. So I immediately stopped using it. Again I expected God to take care of me, but the pain was fully present to the point of nausea. My back was so tense and tight, and it burned with pain between my shoulder blades extending down into my hips. The phantom pain was just as severe. Once again, the constant nagging pain interfered with my daily function. I couldn't stand it any longer, so I entered the office of the chiropractic building nearest my home. I was in tears because of intense and burning back pain. I was desperate and needed pain relief. The chiropractor took X-rays and began treating me. He suggested that I get a prosthetic leg, which would relieve pressure and help align my spine. Technology had greatly improved since my last fitting. I was encouraged with my progress, and I was on my way toward complete healing—spiritual, mental, emotional, and now physical. I set my appointment for a new prosthetic evaluation. I was eager to try to walk again.

Surrendering My Son

Rob has never been a big complainer about pain, even though as a child he had undergone some challenging health concerns of his own. One day he brought to my attention that he was having severe headaches. I initially attributed them to the heat and to the intense workouts and training required for the air force. Daily he was running and disciplining his body to be in tip-top shape, to be fit for basic military training (also known as BMT or boot camp). At any moment, when the call came, he would be leaving for San Antonio, Texas.

But when my son had me feel a lump on the right side of his temple, I freaked out because it was nothing normal. My mind began racing. Thoughts flooded my brain and left me in a temporary state of confusion. With urgency, I told Rob we had to go. I told him to get in the car. "I am taking you in to be seen." He did not hesitate. We arrived at Holland Hospital and went immediately to the emergency department. I felt scared for many reasons. I feared the hospital staff may not evaluate my son because he was a very healthy, extremely fit male, training for the air force and had no healthcare coverage due to the transition from college.

Rob and I did not have to wait long before we were called to come back. The nurse asked a few questions, took my son's vitals, and left the room. A doctor came in next, examined my son, and ordered lab tests and a CT scan. He wanted to get a visual of the bump. As my son and I waited together and discussed life and the situation we found ourselves in, Rob told me he was not worried. He was just hoping to get answers to why he was having these awful headaches. He also expressed how he just wanted to get to boot camp training. All of the individuals who joined the air force at the same time as Rob had already been sent to Texas. My son contacted his sergeant often, seeking answers as to why he was not sent. The sergeant said, "I do not know. There is no reason why you haven't left already." I believed this was an answer to my prayers of keeping my son safe. I also believed that if my son went through boot camp, he would never be the same compassionate man he was. Rob had passed all the physical examinations required to go, including an underwater stamina test, so I believed God had a reason for this delay.

Eventually, Rob was taken back to have the CT scan. While I waited in the room for him to come back, I talked to God. I prayed and prayed. Inside I was a mess. However, I held it together for my son.

Every time I felt my mind wandering to possible outcomes, I prayed and placed my son in God's hands, surrendering him to the only One who could intervene and save him.

I knew that everything happens for a reason, and it's not for me to understand. God knew, and He was in control. My mind went back to my devotional that morning that said to seek contentment in God today and you will be satisfied.

I rolled out into the hallway just to look around and breathe. I called my husband at work to inform him that we were in the emergency room. Minutes felt like hours.

When my son returned, we talked as I held his hand, telling him how much I loved him. We waited some more.

I am not certain if it was a nurse or a doctor who came into the room to notify us that something was visible on the CT scan but more testing was needed. An MRI was being scheduled next. That was a more detailed test which would show a 3D image of the problem area.

At this point, my mind and body were numb. I called my son's father, and Rob notified his girlfriend.

While my son was having the MRI testing, I called Albert again. I knew there were several people on their way to support my son, but I felt alone. God was the only one keeping me. I wheeled back and forth, the equivalent of a person pacing back and forth. I was in and out of the room, up and down the hall, trying to remain calm.

For the second time, I watched as the staff members carefully maneuvered the stretcher back into place, locked the wheels, and exited the room. A nurse came in shortly after, and said, "The lab work came back normal." That was wonderful news. Many more hours passed and then a doctor walked in and revealed both tests showed an abnormal growth in my son's skull. I was devastated. However, a peace was deep within me, knowing God would take care of my son. Whatever the outcome, Rob was in God's hands. I prayed for God's will for my son. In my heart, I already accepted the fact that he may die.

Discharge instructions were given with two additional scheduled appointments. The entire hospital visit was mentally draining and physically exhausting, and I was scheduled for an appointment the next day to do strength-building exercises and practice walking.

Morning arrived. Albert headed off to work, and while Rob slept, I drove to my 8:00 a.m. appointment. I had mixed emotions during this time that I was not sure how to evaluate or process. The neurosurgeon's office that my son was referred to was in the same building as my physical therapy and located just across the hall, so my mind wandered a lot. I have to say, part of me felt numb. However, I had an inner peace, too, that only God can provide. *Thank you, Jesus!*

During this particular PT session, my therapist wanted to go outdoors. We walked together down the hall to the elevator. Once the doors opened, we walked in, and as the doors closed, I was in awe. I was walking! *Twenty-three years* after losing my leg, I was in an elevator, standing . . . no wheelchair in sight. I felt freedom and peace. The elevator doors opened, and we proceeded to walk through the building to the exit doors that led to the back of the building. Once outside, I continued to follow my PT's specific instructions as I walked independently with my prosthetic, only using a cane in my left hand. It was amazing; truly a miracle. I felt joy as I never experienced in that I was putting forth every effort toward my physical therapy, and this time, I was doing it for *me*. Although my left knee burned with pain, I pushed forward. I continued walking around the corner of the building, and I spotted my son's father pulling into the parking lot. Again, I must say, the excitement and joy I experienced are inexplainable. Since before the accident, he had never seen me walk independently. I walked toward him with my physical therapist directly behind me. I said, "Hey, you wanna race?" He smiled and said, "You are gonna make me cry." The delight on his face was priceless. I could see how proud he was of me.

The following afternoon, Rob and I met his father at the brain and spine center. It was a lengthy appointment. The specialist came in and out several times during the evaluation, asking many questions and explaining the upcoming procedure. All I can say is, as the three of us sat together, I had peace. The peace that *only* God can provide.

My son had his parents there with him, by his side to support and love him through this trial. I thank God always for the relationship his dad and I have in placing our son's interest above all. There is no greater joy. We were fulfilling this promise to one another, precisely the parents we planned to be before our son came into this world. We were in this together.

The day of the surgery came, and Rob was admitted to the hospital and underwent a stereotactic craniotomy, a surgery to temporarily remove a section of his skull, for the golf ball–sized growth to be removed and biopsied. The damaged skull section was replaced with hardware. The results came back that it was a benign meningioma. *Thank you, Jesus!*

For the next five days, I remained by my son's side at the hospital and journaled. My son's courage and faith in God left me speechless. Rob inspired me with the peace he brought to our family during this time; it was clear evidence of his trust in God.

Although the following days were heartbreaking and challenging, they were filled with God's provision, peace, and protection. Rob was medically stable and discharged. I was grateful to have him back home. I felt such an inner peace, although I could never have imagined our current situation. I was confident that God answered my prayer of keeping my son safe, and this was no "random" medical issue. I am forever grateful.

When asked to write a few paragraphs for our church newsletter, Rob wrote:

> I was recently baptized in Lake Michigan on June 13. Being baptized was that sure indicator of my faith put in Jesus Christ. After all the things that my family and I have been through, we need faith and Jesus Christ. As some may know, I went to Ferris State University for a while, then decided to join the air force. Almost ready to leave, I was having severe headaches. Came to find out I had a benign meningioma tumor, and now I'm left with five plates and ten screws

in my head. As for the air force, I'm delayed at least six more months and will be limited in job selection. It's all in God's hands, though, so I'm just praying about it. In the meantime, I'm trying to go back to college and soon work my way up to be a chiropractor after the air force. That's my goal, but I can't do it without God.

Once Rob was medically cleared, he returned to his place of employment, resumed his physical training regime, and returned to college. Rob was determined to make the best of his life while he waited to hear back from the air force recruiting office.

Many weeks later, Rob received a letter from the Department of Defense informing him that he had been found permanently disqualified for entry into the armed forces of the United States due to his history of meningioma. My prayers were answered. Although my son was very disappointed, this news only propelled him forward. Rob began searching for a home of his own. Only twenty years old, he applied for a home loan and was approved. I was so very proud of him for persevering.

Rob graduated from Grand Rapids Community College with an associate of arts degree. He then enrolled in a bachelor's program at Grand Valley State University.

At this time our family had been attending services together at Ridge Point Community Church, and on Palm Sunday, my son's fiancée, Chelsea, was baptized. Weeks later, at separate commencements, they both graduated. Rob was accepted into Palmer College of Chiropractic in Port Orange, Florida. To God be all the glory.

Rob and Chelsea set their wedding date following their college graduations. For weeks leading up to this gorgeous and blessed Saturday in June, I was overjoyed yet tearful. When my son requested that I choose a song for our mother-son dance, I searched for the perfect song. As mothers do, I cried tears of joy and rehearsed memories of my little boy who was now a grown man becoming a husband. As we began dancing, I told my son how proud I was of the man he had become. Rob shared with me that I did a wonderful job raising him, and that I could not have done it without both his dad *and* Albert. It was confirmation of God's redemption that brought abundant joy to my heart and buckled my knee. My wheelchair was brought to me, and we finished our dance beautifully. Although there were a few hundred people in attendance, when I was on the dance floor with my son, it felt like we were the only two there. I am grateful that God allowed me to live in the midst of that moment. I treasure my son. I would not be the woman I am today without him. He is truly a gift from God. His obedience in inviting me to church to receive Jesus has literally transformed not only me, but future generations of our family. I had always believed in God, but my life was changed after inviting Jesus to be the Lord of my life. Every question that had weighed so heavily on me for years was all nothing now. I was, and still am, amazed at all the situations God orchestrated to get me to where I am today—for all the people He has impacted through us by simply obeying. God knew where our lives would lead if we were obedient. He alone gets the glory.

God's faithfulness, goodness, mercy, and protection through-out the years are answered prayers for my son's life. Rob graduated from Palmer College of Chiropractic, and six months later, his wife did too. Rob and Chelsea moved back to Michigan and opened their business, Resilience Chiropractic. Although it's an hour drive away, my husband and I are both under Rob's care. The Gonstead approach has completely eliminated the pain between my shoulder blades. As a wheelchair user, that is a miracle!

Seeking God's Face

My faith in the Lord continued to grow stronger, and I was on a mission of seeking God above all. Nothing else mattered. I was caring for my in-laws, attending two Bible studies, one with my husband and another with ladies. I was a Kid's Hope mentor and part of the prayer team at church, but something was holding me back from the fullness of becoming all who God created me to be. I was determined to find out.

Around that same time, a dear friend and sister in Christ, Dawn, invited me to a weekday gathering at a home in Holland to worship and study God's Word. I accepted. I could sense right away God's Spirit was present. I left with an "Inner Healing and Deliverance" pamphlet in my hand, not sure if I would go, but I *was* interested. I received a phone call later that evening asking if I was interested in attending the event by DeGraw Ministries. I found myself saying, "Yes! Absolutely!" almost in desperation. I was definitely curious about the topics listed on the page, such as forgiveness, fear, unworthiness, and rejection. I also received the news someone had already paid for me to attend. It was quite a commitment, as each session was three days in length, but I wanted complete inner healing and deliverance, whatever that looked like. I was committed, expecting to receive whatever healing God had for me, including hidden pain.

The very first evening, it was said that we must deal with unforgiveness. Forgiveness comes before deliverance. *That was it!* My heart started pounding rapidly. Not long ago, I asked God to search my soul and show me what was stopping me from being truly *happy*. Something was missing. It was revealed to me that throughout my life I had been able to forgive *every* individual who hurt me; however, I still had *unforgiveness* in my heart toward myself. The moment I realized this, I prayed to God and asked Him to forgive me for the unforgiveness that I had toward myself. I already knew God forgave me, *but this* was eye-opening. I leaned in and soaked up every word. I digested everything specific to my life, and knew I was exactly where God wanted me to be. After Kathy and her team prayed over me, my prayer language was activated and I began speaking in tongues. The truth permeated my body, and I was never going to be the same. I enjoyed every convicting, truthful topic taught.

Months later, upon acceptance, I was discipled by Kathy. While interning at DeGraw Ministries, I was given many assignments. One in particular was to read a chapter titled, "Loss of a Child." In reading, I came to the realization that I have suffered great loss of my children through abortions, a miscarriage, and the untimely death of my stepdaughter.

As I continued in the chapter, weeping and grieving for my children, I cried uncontrollably for a period of time, and then I repented. I asked God and my children to forgive me for decisions that I had blindly made in selfishness. And I forgave myself too. Immediately, I felt peace and knew one day we would reunite in heaven.

I am forever grateful to Kathy. I learned how to speak out loud, pray, and declare exactly what I was seeking God's help for. Daily, upon waking, I would anoint myself and pray over my body for physical healing, asking God to help me and guide my day. My season of learning at DeGraw Ministries transformed my life.

I am no longer a slave to fear nor a captive burdened with shame or unworthiness. The father of lies has no place in my life. Christ has truly set me free!

Post-abortion trauma is real and manifests in various ways. Many women, and men too, experience depression, deep regrets, guilt, and shame as a result of the choice made amid the lie that abortion offers a way of escape. According to author and speaker Pat Layton, "An estimated 43% of women of childbearing age have had at least one abortion. These women are not necessarily unknown to you. They may be your sisters, your daughters, your friends and even your mothers."[4]

For me shame was a constant companion. Abortion is a decision that affects an entire family, a lifelong heartbreak that only God can heal. God's timing is perfect in *all* things. I trust Him fully as I share my entire life of brokenness with my adult children. If you or someone you know is faced with an unplanned pregnancy, please know there is hope and compassionate help available. For more information and resources, go to www.mypositiveoptions.org.

I am a sinner saved by God's grace and mercy. I have surrendered all that I am to my Lord and Savior and am standing on God's promises. I believe this life is not our own, and we are called to assist others, having been healed by Christ ourselves. I know that I know that I know I am forgiven. I am worthy. God showed me that I did not need to do one more thing for Him. It was by grace and grace alone that I had been saved, not by works (Ephesians 2:8–9).

After eight months of intense physical therapy, and as much as I loved having two feet on the ground and looking people in the eye while talking, I had to admit, I was more disabled wearing the prosthetic leg. I had a deep sense of joy and satisfaction knowing that I had given it my all, but I was not going to push through the excruciating knee and hip pain any longer. I resumed the medical marijuana as needed. I declined a knee replacement, having been diagnosed with osteopenia and osteoporosis. I was treated for five years with three different medications and currently have no need for more, as my bone density has been stable for the last two years. I was proud of myself. I accepted myself fully with one leg, whether using a prosthetic, forearm crutches, my manual wheelchair, or my power wheelchair. I began to see myself through God's eyes. He loved me unconditionally, and I, too, love myself no matter how I present this earthly body to the world. I knew in my heart it was time to except the fact that this, too, was only temporary. I had complete peace. Billy Graham once said, "Our sense of joy, satisfaction, and fulfillment in life increases, no matter what the circumstances, if we are in the center of God's will."[5]

Following Christ does not promise an easy, trial-free life. Many times you will encounter impossible situations. These circumstances will test you and may even cause you to lose hope. But God is asking you to place your trust and faith in Him. When faith is all you have, you realize faith is all you need, because nothing is impossible with God. Jesus says in John 16:33, "I have told you these things, so that in Me you may have [perfect] peace and confidence. In the world you have tribulation and trials and distress and frustration; but be of good cheer [take courage; be confident, certain, undaunted]! For I have overcome the world. [I have deprived it of power to harm you and have conquered it for you]" (AMPC). I have struggles every day. In this life we will suffer, but our hope is in the Lord. Like me, you can also forgive the unthinkable and overcome and have His perfect peace. I am living for the glory of God right where I am—in the daily struggle.

CHAPTER 12

Redeemed for a Thousand Generations

All authority in heaven and on earth has been given to me. Therefore go and make disciples of all nations, baptizing them in the name of the Father and of the Son and of the Holy Spirit, and teaching them to obey everything I have commanded you. And surely I am with you always, to the very end of the age.

Matthew 28:18–20

EVERY SINGLE ONE OF US IS BORN INTO THE WORLD NAKED AND sinful. Some of us are brought up in the church; some of us are not. But we all have one thing in common—generational sin and family dysfunction. It's there. Situations differ from one family to the next, but I can assure you that if you sketched out a family tree, you would see both good and bad patterns. You would also be able to identify similar patterns of sin and also which generation broke the curse of the sin pattern because of faith. Having a faith line in your family tree is something very special.

Deuteronomy 5:9 tells us, "You shall not worship them or serve them; for I, the LORD your God, am a jealous (impassioned) God [demanding what is rightfully and uniquely mine], visiting (avenging) the iniquity (sin, guilt) of the fathers on the children [that is, calling the children to account for the sins of their fathers], to the third and the fourth *generations* of those who hate Me" (AMP). Our God is a jealous God. He wants your heart more than anything. I have wonderful news for you even if you are the only one following after Christ in your family line—you can be the one to unconditionally love your family and friends right into the kingdom of God. As hard as it may seem, and regardless of what you see, if you persevere, wash their feet, encourage them, and refuse to give up on them as Christ never gave up on you, you can be a generation transformer, loving others to Christ, one by one.

One day you and I will stand before our Lord and hope to hear these words, "Well done, good and faithful servant!" (Matthew 25:21). Jesus wants us to tell everyone we know about His love for them, to give them a hope and a future just like the one He has given you. His final instructions are to *go*! Who do you need to share the love of Christ with today? Are you willing?

For the Love of My Father-in-Law, Shorty

On a late September afternoon, on my way home from visiting my best friend Katie, who lives in Indiana, I stopped at my in-laws' home to use the restroom. My father-in-law, who we call Shorty, greeted me as I came inside. I immediately noticed his jeans were wet. I mentioned it to him without causing embarrassment. He said, "It's been happening for a few days, and I don't even feel it." I told him that I would take him to see a doctor in the morning. He agreed to go.

The next morning, I picked up Shorty, who at that time was eighty-seven years old. My mother-in-law, Phyllis, chose to remain home. She had absolutely no interest in going because she already had everything she needed at home. As long as the television was on her channel of choice, she was content. I brought him straight to Holland Hospital. After triage, Shorty was sent directly to the emergency room, where they ran many tests. The physician entered the room and said, "Sir, you had a heart attack." Shorty replied, "No. I didn't feel anything." We were informed that he was now being admitted because he was also in kidney failure. The physician asked about his activities of daily living, who he lived with, and about his health history. When asked about tobacco and alcohol use, he lied. I could not allow Shorty to deceive the medical team who was to care for him, so I spoke up. I told the physician that he drank and smoked daily and had for many decades.

As hard as it was for me knowing Shorty was going to be mad at me, this wasn't the first time I had to share the truth with an emergency physician for him. Years earlier, I brought him in when he was having severe pain, which resulted in his gallbladder being removed. I knew my father-in-law loved me, and he also knew that I cared deeply for him. I loved him enough to endure him being mad at me temporarily.

Unfortunately, we learned that he also had prostate cancer, and a transurethral resection of the prostate (TURP) surgery was scheduled. Shorty was informed that after his procedure, he would be going home with a catheter and needed to abide by a sodium-restricted diet. He was placed on several prescription medications, including nicotine patches.

Phyllis wanted no part in caring for him, for many reasons, but primarily because she was selfish. She didn't know the Lord, so she wasn't much into self-sacrifice at this point. The hospital staff planned to place Shorty in a nursing home because his home was not suitable. Without hesitation, I spoke up and said I would accept responsibility to care for my father-in-law as our home was handicap accessible. Before my life in Christ, I would never have agreed to help with the kind of care involved, but God was working in me and through me. He healed me fully and gifted me with love and compassion to do this work for my father-in-law. Needless to say, Shorty was grateful, and together we humbled ourselves and put aside the embarrassment. The staff taught me the daily routine of how to care for his medical needs.

I knew this was going to be a big task, because on top of everything else, Shorty did not have medical insurance aside from Medicare and VA (Veterans Affairs) benefits. At that time, the VA benefits could only be utilized in a veterans hospital or clinic. He also needed a great deal of help with personal business.

Upon discharge, he was also informed he had cataracts in both eyes and needed to give up his driver's license, which he agreed to do. In-home nursing was scheduled to come and check on him regularly.

During the daytime, I was my father-in-law's caregiver. We spent many hours together driving thousands of miles to and from the VA building to get him established with a physician. I enjoyed that time with my father-in-law. We listened to Crowder on repeat during our lengthy commutes. He came alive when I turned it on and turned it up. I loved looking in my rearview mirror and seeing Shorty singing worship songs by heart. My van was not only a blessing to me; it was a blessing for him too. Entering and exiting the van, he did not have to duck, hence his nickname Shorty. He only had to walk the length of the ramp.

When Albert arrived home from work, he took over caring for his father. At that time, I had been caregiving for my mother-in-law for over seven years and running back and forth to Bloomingdale to help her too. It was all overwhelming. We decided it would be better to have them both move closer to our home, so we applied at an apartment complex for seniors near our home and were placed on a waiting list.

It was hard watching Shorty go through so many life changes, but losing his independence was the hardest. A few days in a row he woke up angry and was unwilling to eat. I immediately shared that with my husband. Albert believed it was related to missing his wife and his home, so he went to pick up his mother. Hesitantly, she agreed to spend one night at our home with him.

God really does work in mysterious ways. Even though caring for my father-in-law was definitely taxing on my husband and me, it also meant he was in our household, watching us live out our faith. Due to the care required, I attended Sunday church services alone. Undoubtedly our life looked very different than he was used to and remembered. He became open to hearing about Jesus. In our living room, Albert led his father to the Lord. Four days later, Albert's brother, Robert, was visiting his father, and he too accepted Christ in our living room. I was in awe. I am still in awe. For fifty-seven days, Shorty lived in our home, feeling more loved and cared for than any other time in his life.

Nine months later, I received approval for my in-laws to move into the apartment located less than two miles from our home. What a relief! My husband and his brother moved their parents. Shortly before the move, my in-laws received a letter stating the Social Security

Administration was going to be directly depositing funds. Because they had never had a checking account, Albert took his parents to the bank to set one up and began taking care of their finances. Although we enjoyed helping them, it was very time consuming, because they relied on us to do *everything*. Robert worked third shift and helped out when he was able. I loved my in-laws, and I enjoyed helping them, but it was my father-in-law who I had a special connection with. Not only was he elderly, but he was a veteran and deserved the respect. He helped me in my time of need, and I was honored to be able to help him too.

After my in-laws were settled into their new place, they began attending church with us, where three months later, my mother-in-law, at sixty-five years old, accepted Christ as her Lord and Savior. Phyllis was baptized, Shorty reaffirmed his faith, and they became members. Our family was coming to the Lord, one by one, and we were in awe. We are still in awe. There is nothing more important than to see our loved ones lifted out of the pit of hell and transformed by God's love— His unconditional, life-giving love. Before Christ, my father-in-law was hard, only kind when drinking. After inviting Christ back into his life, he became so gentle and generous. I was blessed to know him before conversion because I could see the drastic change in him. Truly, miracles happen every day, and he was certainly one of them. I am so grateful for what the Lord has done in our family.

During this time, I was also working with our church in a leadership capacity, meeting and assisting individuals in their times of need by various means. I would pray with them in person, over the phone, or during a hospital visit. I would meet them for coffee and have face-to-face conversations, offering resources as needed. It was the beginning of a new year, and my husband and I went into a time of prayer and fasting. A few items were highlighted to us, one being that I must take steps for my health first and foremost. I wrote to our church leadership thanking them for trusting me with the opportunity in shepherding others, but I was stepping away. This season of my life was a time to focus on myself and family.

It was also revealed that I was to delegate and fully transfer the care of my in-laws to their sons. After nine years of them living near us and a few falling incidents, it was time for more help. After a family meeting, we decided to move them in with their son, Robert. I established in-home nursing care. I am grateful for the many years of assisting them and getting them to a place of health. I love them dearly. Seven months later, while our family was celebrating Shorty's ninety-sixth birthday, he had a stroke. He was hospitalized for forty-eight hours and bounced back miraculously. One month later, he died in his sleep, peacefully. He had nine amazing years as a Christian and lived out the remaining years of his life much differently than he would have otherwise. He would have died in shame and regret, very sick, and without support or care from his wife. But because of his new life in Christ, he died with respect, in peace, and with his loved ones surrounding him. He was respected, loved, and will be greatly missed. Our family rejoices knowing we will reunite with him in heaven.

A Daughter to Call My Own

Albert and I were so heartbroken for his daughter Heather after Jeanie's death, for obvious reasons, but especially when we learned that she was not allowed to talk about her sister at her mother's home. This was traumatizing for Heather. She often turned to food for comfort. During her high school years, she became even more detached.

Albert and I encouraged Heather to talk about her feelings when she came to visit us on the weekends, but she never wanted to. She would rather curl up with a blanket and read a book.

We gave her the grace to talk when she felt ready. Little did we know it would be over five years before she would comfortably talk about Jeanie, and even then, it was minimal.

During Heather's senior year, she moved in with her maternal grandmother, because her mother and stepfather moved two hours away. Albert and I were so proud of her, as she, too, like my son Rob, was a second-generation high school graduate. Our hearts were filled with joy as we watched her make decisions which led to her independence as a young woman. Heather worked her way up into management at the restaurant she worked at, moved into her own apartment, and began dating. Two years later, our grandson was born.

One late fall day, Albert received an unexpected phone call. Heather's boyfriend, the father of her son, called to ask for Albert's blessing in marrying his daughter. It was respectful, and Albert was grateful. Shortly after that, Heather asked me if I would officially be the "mother of the bride." It had been many years since Heather had any form of contact or relationship with her own mother. I cried. I was humbled and graciously accepted, but I was absolutely terrified of what exactly that meant. My husband's work schedule had just changed. He was only working four days a week, so that made me nervous. I never had a wedding or any kind of reception, so I had no clue of what to do. I shared the wonderful news with the ladies in my weekly Bible study, and they offered their time to assist me. I was thankful. My friend Kate selflessly assisted me in all the preparations needed to have a beautiful wedding and reception. Our daughter's wedding was blessed. She now had a stepdaughter to call her own too.

At the end of that evening, Heather's grandmother approached Albert and me with tears in her eyes. She turned to me and said, "Thank you for being a real mother to Heather as my daughter was not capable. She is not well." I was completely taken by surprise but replied, "I love her. Thank you." Albert and I drove home with such a wonderful gift of gratitude knowing that we were respected and that God knew every moment of our struggles throughout the years. He made it known to us that evening, through it all, we were appreciated. Only by the grace of God. Albert and I were grateful to see another generational sin pattern broken. Our grandson had married parents who would become an example for him.

On and off throughout the years, we invited Heather and her family to join us at church, and on a few occasions they did. Our grandson was excited about Jesus. When he came to spend the weekend with us, he requested that I read *The Jesus Storybook Bible*. In one weekend, we read through it, morning, noon, and night, until it was finished. Albert and I were filled with joy knowing that his little heart was hungry for more. Heather wanted to begin attending church but did not know where to go. My husband and I suggested she check out the church where my son and his wife attended. She agreed. And for a few months, Albert and I attended church as a family with our adult children and grandkids too. What a blessing that was. Our first family attendance was on Easter, and when the invitation was given to accept Christ as Lord and Savior, Heather raised her hand. My eyes were filled with tears. She accepted the One who truly brings comfort. My husband and I were obedient to God's leading, being flexible enough to attend a different church with our adult children for a season, and we were rewarded. God allowed us to be present and witness our daughter being welcomed into the family of God. Although Heather's husband has not made that choice yet, we love him regardless. And we know because of Jesus, there is *always* hope. Our family prays for his salvation and for his heart to soften and turn to the Lord because Jesus loves him more than any one of us possibly could.

Placing My Sister, Amy, into His Hands

From the moment my little sister was born, I loved her and helped her whenever I could. But sadly, throughout Amy's life, she suffered from deep insecurities and made many poor choices. Amy dated a few boys but ended up in an abusive relationship that nearly cost her life. Amy was following in our mother's footsteps, bound by the generational curse of bad relationships and abuse, and I did not know how to help.

Amy struggled daily with her alcoholism but did ask God to help her. We talked frequently on the phone, and I visited her when our schedules permitted, which meant when she was sober enough to allow me to come over to her home. I felt helpless. On my sister's birthday, Albert and I visited her briefly. Due to her home being cluttered, I was not able to get through the mess on crutches safely. She came outside. We hugged, and I told her how much I loved her. I told her I couldn't continue to worry myself sick over her addictions and watch her destroy herself with alcohol. I simply asked her to repeat the sinner's prayer and invite Jesus into her heart. She did. That was a huge release for me. Before we left, my husband took a picture of Amy and me as we stood side by side. She and I hugged again, and I left peaceful, knowing she was in God's hands.

Amy rapidly declined. Each time I spoke to her, it was evident she was unaware of time and her reality was distorted. I felt an urgency to go visit her, so I drove to her home. I sat in the driveway and beeped the horn while calling her cell phone. Sam, her boyfriend, answered her phone. I said, "Put Amy on the phone." He was very controlling and often would tell me that she was drunk or sleeping. Amy got on the phone, and I told her to come outside. I needed to see her. She said, "I cannot walk." I asked her to put Sam back on the phone. I told him to help Amy outside. He refused. I told him if he didn't help her outside that I was calling 911. Immediately, he said, "Okay," and he brought her outside. Upon laying my eyes on my sister, I knew she was not well. I had Sam assist Amy into the front seat of my van. I drove her straight to Zeeland Community Hospital where she was evaluated, admitted, and placed in the intensive care unit. Her potassium was dangerously low. I was informed her heart might stop at any moment. Amy had cirrhosis of the liver, pneumonia, and ascites (excess fluid in her abdomen). She had to endure an abdominal paracentesis procedure to release fluid from her belly. Amy was placed on antibiotics and intravenous fluids and watched closely. For the next several days, I sat by my sister's bedside while Sam remained home.

I explained to the hospital staff that Amy had suffered a closed head injury previously. She was in an abusive, codependent, and neglectful relationship, and Sam was her "caregiver." It fell on deaf ears.

While Amy was inpatient, her unemployed boyfriend who lived in her home, used her disability check to fund his addictions. Amy was transferred to a nursing home for rehabilitation to relearn how to walk due to the neuropathy in her legs. She was thirty-five years old and discharged using a four-wheeled walker. She was still so young.

Sometimes people who call on the name of the Lord to help them actually get worse before they get better. You may have noticed that for yourself in someone you know and love, but God is always working whether we see the evidence or not. I was determined to do whatever was necessary to see my sister healthy and whole; little did I know my prayers were coming full circle, and God had a plan to use me all along.

A few years passed, and I hadn't been able to talk to Amy since she called me on my birthday. Sam "allowed" her to use her own cell phone briefly. After that I didn't speak to my sister for over three months. Because it was winter, we didn't see one another due to the lack of snow removal in her driveway. I was unable to visit. Each time I called her cell phone, Sam would answer it and say that she was passed out drunk or sleeping. I felt my hands were tied. I continually prayed for God to intervene in their situation.

It was a late winter evening, and I was in bed sleeping when I received two phone calls back-to-back from different phone numbers. One left a voicemail. I sat up in bed and listened to it. It was Sam calling to inform me that Amy was sick and was being airlifted to Spectrum Butterworth and next of kin was asked to be there. I shared the news with my husband and told him I had to go. I quickly got dressed and speedily drove to Grand Rapids. Upon my arrival, I went to the emergency department and told them I was there to see my sister. I was the only person there. Sam did not show up. Once the physician talked with me, I was informed Adult Protective Services was going to be involved. I was grateful. I told the staff that I had been trying for years to reveal the severity of her life situation but nobody took it seriously until that moment.

Amy, then thirty-eight, was on life support due to pulmonary failure. She had pneumonia and sepsis and was unresponsive. The drug screen test revealed she had Norco, marijuana, and methamphetamines in her bloodstream. She was hooked up to a machine to check brain activity. It appeared she had not showered for months. I prayed and asked God to give me the strength to endure this trial to assist my sister. Although I was heartbroken, I had peace because God is faithful. I remained by Amy's side. I prayed and fasted for her life. I journaled too. There were many professionals involved within the first few hours.

I was experiencing information overload, but I was willing to do whatever necessary to keep my sister safe from that moment forward, if in fact she survived. I sent a text to my life-group leader and asked for prayer. Two hours later, she came to the hospital to sit with me.

After speaking with the medical social worker and Adult Protective Services, I was asked specifically what my concerns were. One of the many concerns I shared was that my sister's disability check would soon be deposited and that Sam would use the funds while she was inpatient. I was sent to Ottawa County probate court and granted an emergency temporary guardianship to freeze her assets. Days later, when Amy's check was deposited, a request was made to transfer one thousand dollars of the money to another account, only to be denied due to the quick action taken to protect her.

Ten days after being granted temporary guardianship, at a hearing with Sam present, I gained full guardianship and conservatorship.

Sam continuously harassed me. Adult Protective Services assisted me in responding to him, and due to the severity of Amy's medical situation, they moved her to another floor. No information was given to anyone who called. In fact, the hospital would not acknowledge that she was a patient. They advised me to change my phone number and to obtain personal protection orders (PPOs) on both of us, so I did.

I became representative payee for my sister's disability. Once that was in place, I opened a conservator checking account and had her funds directly deposited. I was then able to pay past-due utilities. Amy's property taxes were delinquent, and she did not have money to pay them. I hired a lawyer for assistance.

I took steps to evict Sam, but he physically destroyed the home in the process. Amy's neighbors contacted me several times when they heard the wreckage taking place. I was granted the PPOs for Amy and myself, so when the police were called to the home, Sam was served.

At one of the hearings, Sam requested the PPOs be dismissed, but the judge ruled that they would stand. She clearly told him, with his family in attendance, that he must stop harassing and stalking us. But it fell on deaf ears.

The situation intensified due to him and others using and manufacturing methamphetamines. My sister's house was the squatter's house for those who did drugs regularly.

I reestablished Amy's car-accident insurance claim to pay for accident-related injuries and applied for Michigan Medicaid. I diligently worked to establish all that was necessary and involve professionals while my sister was miraculously improving, *slowly*. Once again, God sustained her life.

Amy was discharged from Spectrum Butterworth Hospital, and on Good Friday, my husband and I transported her to a subacute rehab facility, Grace of Douglas. Before Amy was admitted, the medical social worker and I spoke with the director of nursing about a no-contact/no-information order. We needed that in place against Sam, his mother, and his sister. The facility was the nearest one to my home, so I could continue to see her daily. Although that was a temporary environment, it's what was recommended due to her health. Amy was weak and needed to heal and improve more and learn how to walk again.

I began taking Amy to church with our family, and on Father's Day, she was baptized. My sister was the very first individual to enter the baptismal tub at Third Coast Community Church. At Amy's request, I invited her favorite uncle and his family, who are believers, to attend. It was a memorable day.

Initially, my sister was safe, but after a breakdown in communication with staff, Amy gained access to a phone. Sam learned where she was located. His mother enabled the situation by driving him to the facility. His sister entered the facility, and chaos ensued.

On a beautiful July evening, Albert and I joined our life group in downtown Saugatuck to listen to the live music in the park; we left our cell phones home. It was a pleasant and well-deserved evening that was short-lived.

I arrived home and checked my phone. I had several missed phone calls and voice mails from the nursing home facility and the local police department. My heart began rapidly pounding inside my chest.

When I returned the first phone call, I was so upset I could hardly breathe. Within five minutes, a police officer arrived. I was informed Amy was missing and the nursing home had called the police and given them detailed information about the car that she was physically carried to. Allegan County Central Dispatch had my sister listed as missing and endangered. I was overwhelmed. The officer asked me if I had any idea of where they might go. I was unsure. I gave him Amy's cell phone number because Sam always had her phone. The officer called it, but it went to voice mail, so he had central dispatch contact the phone carrier and ping that phone. It pinged to a location in the next county over. A deputy with the Ottawa County Sheriff's Department notified us that they had located a male, possibly Sam, who came outside of that residence and appeared to be hanging a camera. After several hours, the deputies entered that home and located Amy in the basement. Sam had carried Amy down a flight of stairs, set her on a couch, and gave her cigarettes and a lighter and liquor. One of the deputies handcuffed Sam and placed him in custody. Sam then said, "I knew this day would come. It had to be done. I needed her to be out of that place so we could be together. She just isn't safe there." Sam was transported to the Allegan County jail where he was charged with kidnapping and unlawful imprisonment.

Amy was transported by ambulance to Holland Hospital for a medical evaluation. I met them at the hospital. My sister was highly intoxicated. Her blood alcohol level was twice the limit. I waited in the ER hallway due to her explosive behavior. Amy's heart rate was fast, blood pressure low, and she was hooked up to an IV for fluids. Hours passed until she was capable of speaking clearly. Once my sister was medically cleared for discharge, I assisted her from the hospital wheelchair into my van and buckled her in. I drove her back to Grace of Douglas, and waiting for me were two of my life-group friends. Upon approaching the building, the director of nursing, who prearranged all safety measures originally, approached me and looked me in the eye and said, "Amy cannot be a resident here." I was overwhelmed and in shock because this was the facility where I believed Amy would be safe and fully taken care of due to all the safety measures in place. I was wrong.

For the next several hours, while my friends remained with Amy in a waiting room, I along with the staff, desperately called around looking for another nursing facility that would accept my sister. The first place that had an opening was the facility I transported her to; it was an hour farther drive for me. Sam was eventually released and repeatedly violated the PPOs. His family found my sister once again and harassed the new facility to the point of the police being called.

It's a long, ugly story, but as of this writing, Sam is incarcerated on several charges of controlled substance possession. According to the Michigan Department of Corrections status, his minimum sentence is two years and ten months, and maximum sentence, twenty years. His sister has since died in a car accident. The harassment has ceased.

In the midst of the chaos, I pressed on to get my sister the professional assistance she needed. God sustained me and strengthened me throughout. When I gained custody of my sister, she weighed only eighty-eight pounds. She is now 125 pounds and walking. Amy lives independently. She works part-time and volunteers. She is sober and loves life. We see each other regularly, and she continually showers me with gratitude in helping her. We both give all the glory to God.

I am pleased to say that in 319 days of sacrificial love and tears, I was able to accomplish every task that I set out to achieve to get my sister to a place of health, wholeness, and safety. God had answered my prayers. I resigned guardianship/conservatorship and transferred all to a professional. As hard as it was, it is truly a miracle to see the woman of God she is today. Amy and I both pray for the individuals from her past. We pray they seek God with all their hearts and be transformed. I have a loving, kind, and compassionate sister, and I would not change a thing. Only God could have orchestrated every critical detail that would save my sister's life.

Never give up on those you love because God is relentless in drawing those He calls, even when His timing is not necessarily our own. Never in a million years would I have ever predicted the salvation of these family members. I am a witness to what can happen to a person when they put aside their lost and wayward living and put on a new life in Christ. I've seen firsthand when family members, who were on the brink of physical death, turned to spiritual health and wholeness and complete healing. I've seen firsthand how stubborn, hard hearts were transformed into compassionate ones. I've seen greed turn to generosity. I've seen selfishness turn to selflessness, chronic complaining turn to enjoying the moment, decades of addictions broken, joy replacing anger, blaming turn to acceptance, unforgiveness released, and poverty turn into more than enough. I've seen the Bible be opened in search for answers instead of returning to old habits. I could go on and on, but seeing those I love on the brink of physical death become renewed to spiritual life continues to amaze me. I will always be amazed at what God has done. I acknowledge that answering the call to help those family members or friends in need is not easy, and it's even back-breaking, but you never know what God will do through you for them.

To God Be All the Glory

I ALWAYS THANK GOD THAT HE KNOWS ME BETTER THAN I KNOW myself. For years, I wanted a maple tree planted outside in my front yard. The beauty of a new season in the life of a tree brings me so much hope and peace. Watching the new growth in the spring bloom into a green shade covering for outdoor enjoyment is absolutely amazing, but even more so is the majestic beauty of the leaves changing colors into red, orange, and yellow during the fall. It leaves me breathless year after year and with great expectation for the beauty of yet another season. There were many costly attempts to grow our own maple trees, but each was unsuccessful. The trees died due to lack of nourishment.

One Maundy Thursday, Albert invited me to join him out back on our property where he was clearing up some fallen debris. As I took in the beauty of the new season, I was slowly riding on my scooter around the yard, and my husband revealed a very established, beautiful maple tree. I was overjoyed! And then he directed my attention to another one, much smaller in size but equally healthy and vibrant. I praised God for His promises. My maple grove was established. It's as if He gave us a double portion for our former troubles. I felt God's deep love and approval as I briefly thought back to the life of the curse but now a life of blessing. Our family tree is being filled with people who love the Lord too.

The Lord led me to this land, and He continually blesses our family with it. His timing is always perfect. I am blessed beyond measure.

Oh my goodness, I have faced many difficult truths. Honestly, I did my best to face each one with courage, not knowing exactly where it would lead, but doing so with hope, knowing that God is in control. I pressed on because I knew how miserable I was and wanted to be restored to wellness. I didn't realize how broken I was or how many layers had to be peeled off me to get to the core (truth). All I can say is, "Thank you, Jesus," for carrying me all those years. I am grateful for Holy Spirit conviction and discipline. I am nothing without Christ.

It has not been easy. Change did not take place overnight. Ours has been a grace-filled journey, one in which Albert and I radically changed our behavior, breaking the bondage of many familial, generational curses forever. Deuteronomy 7:9 assures us, "Know therefore that the LORD your God is God; he is the faithful God, keeping his covenant of love to a thousand generations of those who love him and keep his commandments." He is faithful.

To this day, I still have limitations and struggles that only some can truly identify with. I have many chronic pain issues throughout my body due to the injuries sustained so long ago, but one day I will have a new body. While I wait for that glorious day, I regularly have chiropractic adjustments, medical massages, aquatic therapy, and physical therapy exercises. When needed, I use medicinal marijuana and CBD oil, as well as a portable TENS unit. All of these mitigate the physical pain, but nothing removes it fully.

I am not perfect; I know this full well. However, I strive daily to be obedient. Christ saved me, cleansed me, transformed me, and redeemed me. I know how to live in the world, and I know how to walk in the Spirit and live life with purpose. My purpose is to glorify God in all I say and do. Intimacy with Jesus, my Lord and Savior, is the number one priority in my life. My life is not my own. *To God be all the glory.*

Albert and I will be celebrating nineteen years of marriage soon, and we are genuinely happy. God has redeemed us and restored our lives abundantly. He has renewed joy and laughter in us through great pain and sorrow. We are blessed that both of our married adult children are expecting children this fall. Everything we have is from the Lord.

Our family has a unique situation, but none of it was a surprise to God. We are proud to share the love of God with others and extend the grace and forgiveness He offers. Without God at the center of our lives, we would not be able. *He alone gets all the glory.*

And we know [with great confidence] that God [who is deeply concerned about us] causes all things to work together [as a plan] for good for those who love God, to those who are called according to His plan and purpose.

Romans 8:28 AMP

Dear one, you are His beloved. I want to encourage you to never give up, even if you are the only one you know following Christ. I encourage you to live out your faith, and love like Jesus. Hope changes everything! I encourage you to let go of all things that bind you, to open up and share your secrets and shame, because exposing them into the light can heal. God will use your story of redemption to help others, you can be sure of that. You'll never know who or when someone will step out from the darkness and into the light, so don't give up. Defeat is not an option. You have the ability to choose between heaven or hell, life or death, blessings or curses. Deuteronomy 30:19 tells us to choose life. The One who holds your destiny is faithful.

The LORD, the LORD, the compassionate and gracious God, slow to anger, abounding in love and faithfulness, maintaining love to thousands, and forgiving wickedness, rebellion and sin.

Exodus 34:6–7

Look what can happen when one person is obedient, when one person turns to Christ, invites others, and witnesses. An entire family, generations, have been turned around to be saved by God. What happened to my family is truly an amazing miracle. We now have hope for future generations—the Bible says for thousands—all because we were obedient. What I learned about breaking generational sin is that it takes humility, courage, and boldness to allow Christ to transform every area that needs healing and restoration, but He will give you the grace one moment at a time. I sit back now and marvel at what God has done. We are a family transformed and redeemed. With God, you, too, can be the one to save your family from hell, restoring them from lives of scorn and shame, disgrace and decline, to an eternal life with Jesus, where peace, joy, and a new sense of purpose and security reign.

Beloved, I pray for your perseverance and victory in overcoming any obstacles. May you have the courage to never give up on those whom you love. God loves you, and so do I. Your life is not your own. *To God be all the glory.*

Ready for a New Life?

If you've read through this entire book and haven't made Jesus the Lord of your life, I personally invite you to do so today. God says in Romans 10:9 that if we make Jesus Lord of our lives and believe He was raised from the dead, we will be saved. Are you ready for a new life? Would you like to receive God's forgiveness and begin a personal relationship with Him? Pray this simple prayer out loud:

> Jesus, I know that I have sinned. I have made many poor choices, and I am in need of a Savior. I am sorry for the way I lived, please forgive me. I believe that when you went to the cross, you went there for me and my sins. I believe you died and rose from the dead. I trust you to save me right now. I surrender my life to you. Thank you for loving me and never giving up on me. Today I know I'm saved, born again, completely forgiven. Help me to live for you every day. In Jesus' name I pray, amen.

If you just prayed that prayer, let me welcome you into God's family. You are loved. I encourage you to seek out others you may know who call Jesus Lord and tell them of your decision. In fact, I would personally love to hear from you. See my contact information near the end of this book. Find a local church who believes the Bible is true, and get yourself a readable Bible to begin reading on your own. A couple of versions I can recommend are the *New International Version* (NIV) and the *New King James Version* (NKJV). Read faithfully each and every day to hear God's message and guidance for you. I encourage you to talk to God, share *everything* with Him. Pray and thank Him for sustaining you and loving you unconditionally. Beloved, enjoy the good life Jesus died to give you.

Other Resources

The Holy Bible
New International Version (NIV)
New King James Version (NKJV)

Inner Healing and Deliverance
Resources by Neil T. Anderson:
The Bondage Breaker: Overcoming Negative Thoughts, Irrational Feelings, Habitual Sins
Victory over the Darkness: Realize the Power of Your Identity in Christ
www.freedominchrist.com
Resources by Kathy DeGraw:
Unshackled: Breaking the Strongholds of Your Past to Receive Complete Deliverance
Prophetic Spiritual Warfare (Podcast)
www.kathydegrawministries.org
Resources by Joyce Meyer:
Battlefield of the Mind: Winning the Battle in Your Mind
Change Your Words, Change Your Life: Understanding the Power of Every Word You Speak
Do Yourself a Favor . . . Forgive: Learn How to Take Control of Your Life Through Forgiveness
How to Hear from God: Learn to Know His Voice and Make Right Decisions
Living Beyond Your Feelings: Controlling Emotions so They Don't Control You
Power Thoughts: 12 Strategies to Win the Battle of the Mind
The Secret Power of Speaking God's Word

Enjoying Everyday Life (TV program)
www.joycemeyer.org

Prayer Books
Draw the Circle: The 40 Day Prayer Challenge by Mark Batterson
Prayers that Rout Demons: Prayers for Defeating Demons and Overthrowing the Power of Darkness by John Eckhardt
Speak Out: Releasing the Power of Declaring Prayer by Kathy DeGraw

Unplanned Pregnancy
www.mypositiveoptions.org

Addictions
www.celebraterecovery.com
www.teenchallengeusa.org

Disability Rehabilitation and Resources
www.joniandfriends.org
www.maryfreebed.com

Sexual Abuse
www.rainn.org
National Sexual Assault Hotline: 800.656.HOPE (4673)

Marriage and Family
Marriage on the Rock by Jimmy Evans
Staying Power: Building a Stronger Marriage When Life Sends Its Worst by Carol & Gene Kent and Cindy & David Lambert

About the Author

Tracy Michaud is a survivor. She is a woman with bold courage and great perseverance. For more than a decade she experienced emotional and sexual abuse, parental rejection, and neglect. She was involved in a deadly car accident, which left her hospitalized for over a year due to life-threatening injuries and an amputation. Since childhood, Tracy has endured numerous life-altering tragedies; but nothing has changed her smile. She is an overcomer. Tracy loves Jesus and is passionate about helping people. She is a dedicated wife, loving mother, and blessed grandmother, who lives in West Michigan with her husband, Albert, and their two Chihuahuas. Tracy enjoys spending quality time with her family. She also enjoys biking on her custom-made hand cycle, swimming, kayaking, going on long drives with no destination in mind, and watching the sunset year-round on Lake Michigan.

To contact Tracy, visit www.tracymichaud.com.

Tracy Michaud
PO Box 26
Fennville, MI 49408

Connect on social media @TracyJMichaud

Notes

Chapter 1

1. "Infants [who] are exposed to secondhand smoke are more likely to be hospitalized for pneumonia during their first year of life than babies who live in non-smoking households. Smoking is also linked to infections of the lower respiratory tract (the lungs and lower airways) in infants under 18 months, which can require hospitalization." "Protecting Infants and Children from Secondhand Smoke," Health Alliance Plan of Michigan, accessed June 16, 2021, www.hap.org/health/smoking/infants.php.

Chapter 5

2. "Teen sues dead dad after crash" *Weekly World News*, August 9, 1988.

Chapter 8

3. Reinhold Niebuhr, quoted in *Alcoholics Anonymous*, 4th ed., (New York: Alcoholics Anonymous World Services, Inc., 2001)

Chapter 11

4. Pat Layton, *A Surrendered Life* (Grand Rapids: Baker Books, 2014), introduction.

5. Billy Graham, *Unto the Hills: A Daily Devotional* (Nashville: W Publishing Group, 1996), 10.

ORDER INFORMATION

To order additional copies of this book, please visit
www.redemption-press.com.
Also available on Amazon.com and BarnesandNoble.com
or by calling toll-free 1-844-2REDEEM.